Managing with Sense and Sensitivity

Christer Sandahl • Mia von Knorring

Managing with Sense and Sensitivity

Professionalism in Leadership

Foreword by Amy C. Edmondson

Springer

Christer Sandahl
Department of Learning, Informatics,
Management and Ethics (LIME)
Karolinska Institutet
Stockholm, Sweden

Mia von Knorring
Department of Learning, Informatics,
Management and Ethics (LIME)
Karolinska Institutet
Stockholm, Sweden

ISBN 978-3-031-24108-6 ISBN 978-3-031-24109-3 (eBook)
https://doi.org/10.1007/978-3-031-24109-3

This Springer imprint is published by the registered company Springer Nature Switzerland AG
The registered company address is: Gewerbestrasse 11, 6330 Cham, Switzerland

Foreword

I am honored to be asked to write a foreword for this important, well-researched, and surprisingly useful book, now being published in English for the first time. Christer Sandahl and Mia von Knorring are serious scholars who bring depth of expertise in organizational psychology and managerial leadership to their collaborative work. I benefitted greatly from the time I spent reading this manuscript, and I am confident that you will as well.

Leadership has never been more important than it is today. More than ever before, organizations confront problems for which off-the-shelf solutions are lacking. Unclear, tension-filled, shifting notions of what needs to be done create the need to organize people and organizations in new ways, but a set of widely taken-for-granted assumptions about how to manage make this difficult. The remarkable achievements of the industrial era have left their mark on every aspect of society, but one of its more subtle vestiges can be found in how people approach the task of managing others. For instance, many managers still believe that if people are slightly afraid of them, and of the consequences of falling short in reaching a target, they will work harder and do better work. This assumption proves a poor fit with the nature of most work today.

Extensive research demonstrates that fear limits cognitive capacity. More specifically, interpersonal fear in managerial relationships leads to far more undesired than desired outcomes. Fear inhibits the very behaviors that are so vital to excellence in the face of uncertainty and thorny tensions. For instance, interpersonal fear in hospitals inhibits the error reporting that is essential for patient safety and quality improvement – and, as I explore in my book *The Fearless Organization: Creating Psychological Safety for Learning, Innovation and Growth*, numerous studies show that psychological safety – defined as a state of low interpersonal fear – enables learning and performance in teams across industries and sectors.

Most work today is knowledge work, which invariably brings uncertainty and problems and requires teamwork and collaboration to develop effective solutions. When people are afraid to speak up with questions, observations, concerns, and mistakes, problems go unsolved, and innovation and performance suffer. For these reasons and more, a new set of managerial competencies is needed to create the conditions where people can perform, collaborate, solve problems, and wrestle with tensions in a productive way. These competencies are not just cognitive but rather primarily emotional and relational.

This is why this book is important. Its treatment of the role of emotions and how challenging it is for most people to manage their own and others' emotions effectively provides useful insights for scholars and practitioners alike. The emotional challenges of management are particularly salient for those managers with people above and below them in an organizational hierarchy (that is to say, nearly all managers), who thereby struggle in the face of the conflicting demands their roles involve. It is not an overstatement to say that learning to manage one's own emotions may be the single most important managerial competency one must develop, a core premise of this book. That this competency remains rare in the modern workplace shows us how much work remains to be done for scholars and practitioners alike, but especially for those in organizations who train and coach managers.

Other managerial assumptions that this book helps us revise include the idea that managers bring answers rather than questions and are primarily tasked with evaluation rather than enabling. Going forward, managers who appreciate their lack of omniscience, nurture their own and others' curiosity, and respond to bad news with equanimity and empathy, rather than frustration or disdain, are those who will help all of us navigate the challenging times ahead. These managers will have both sense and sensitivity.

What Christer and Mia explain so well is that managers must learn to challenge their own belief – far too widely held – that they lack the power or influence to handle the situations their role brings. The authors carefully introduce readers to the ways in which influence *can* be exerted by managers to alter the course of events. They argue that the essence of leading in a managerial role is the responsible handling of emotions. The more you think about this, the more profound this statement becomes. It means that self-awareness and situation awareness in equal measure – to help managers discern when pausing to be as thoughtful and measured as humanly possible – matters a great deal (and also when it doesn't).

This book is useful in that it directly addresses the practical challenges of management, particularly mastering the emotional labor of being a manager. Although these are difficult skills to develop, I believe there is much in the pages ahead to help you do just that. The world continues to become more complex and uncertain. Christer and Mia show that managerial leadership is accordingly about learning and helping others learn. I am confident you will benefit from their thoughtful perspective and research.

Cambridge, MA, USA Amy C. Edmondson

Endorsements

A thoughtful and illuminating analysis of the nature and purpose(s) of leadership and management in contemporary organisations. By placing a focus on meaning and emotions at the core of the book, the authors skilfully articulate a deeply sensitive and embodied approach that recognises our humanity and interdependence, which will resonate with readers from a wide range of backgrounds.

Richard Bolden, Professor of Leadership and Management, Bristol Business School, University of West England, United Kingdom

Realizing what infuses meaning and purpose into a team is fundamental for sustained success. In a world of ever-increasing complexity, this task has become more and more challenging for leaders and managers. This book gives a comprehensive understanding of the intricate web of psychological drivers and blockers that any successful leader needs to be aware of. My only regret is that this book wasn't around earlier in my career. Buy it, read it, and most importantly, reflect deeply on it!

Per-Anders Ericsson, Regional Manager, Skanska Sweden AB, Gothenburg

Managing with Sense and Sensitivity is an outstanding, important, and timely book in the vast field of leadership publications. With a solid foundation in recent research the authors explore and guide the reader through the fields of emotional challenges in leadership, how to understand emotions in leadership situations, and how to handle the demanding leadership situations that are part of daily work of leaders. Leadership is addressed as a collaborative process, to explore how leader's act with others in the ever changing, various situations that evolves in contemporary organizations. This well written book will serve as support and provide insights and reflections for leaders and co-workers alike. Additionally, it will serve as a cornerstone for students of leadership and management in many different disciplines.

Ulla Eriksson-Zetterquist, Professor of Management Studies and Director of Gothenburg Research Institute, Sweden, and Member of the Royal Swedish Academy of Engineering Sciences

This invaluable book guides leaders and managers toward recognizing emotions in ourselves and others as essential information in any work context. By integrating research and wide-ranging theories, e.g., systems thinking, neurobiology, management practices, group dynamics, and role constructs, the authors widen our perspectives on how to use feeling *and* reason in developing oneself as a leader and in developing the teams we lead. This book supports leaders moving beyond theories of management to integrating ideas of management (sense) with the emotional knowing and emotions (sensitivity) that all leaders and teams experience. This thoughtful book will be thought-provoking for any leader who takes it to heart and uses it to explore their own leadership resources by engaging with these writings to open a door into a journey of reflection, curiosity and ongoing development as a leader.

Susan Gantt, Chair, Systems-Centered Training and Research Institute, Emeritus Faculty, Department of Psychiatry and Behavioral Sciences, Emory University School of Medicine, Atlanta, USA

Modest and thoughtful, practical and reflective! This book mirrors the personalities and professional experience of the authors. Their varied and extensive, first-hand knowledge of leadership is used to guide the reader towards discovering and developing his or her own authentic role as manager. It is, in a word, essential reading.

David Gutmann, Executive Chair, Praxis International and Executive Vice President, International Forum for Social Innovation (IFSI), Paris, France

I appreciated this book, especially the way the authors describe how emotions actually are the prerequisite for sound judgement. Some learnings I will apply in my own leadership is to use reflection as a tool to continue to grow as a leader and to be more aware of how my own emotions affect my decisions. I would recommend anybody who is curious and eager to take their leadership skills to the next level to read this book – it provides an understanding of how feelings and reasoning interplay in the modern leadership role.

Karin Rådström, Member of the Board of Management of Daimler Truck Holding AG and CEO of Mercedes-Benz Trucks, Stuttgart, Germany

Managing with Sense and Sensitivity is a rare piece of writing. It is an amalgamation between an academic textbook, a source for personal reflection and self-understanding, and a manual for efficient and human-centric leadership. Christer Sandahl and Mia von Knorring manage to identify the key levers of leadership and help us understand the world we live in. It is a must-read for anyone who wants to understand how organizations define our lives, how leadership works on the societal level, and what makes humans take the actions they do. It provides views that make us see the world from new, intriguing perspectives. Please, read it!

Lars Strannegård, Professor, Bo Rydin & SCA Chair of Leadership; President, Stockholm School of Economics

Contents

About the Authors

Christer Sandahl is Psychologist, and Professor Emeritus of Social and Behavioural Sciences at Karolinska Institutet, a medical university in Stockholm, Sweden, and has extensive experience as a business consultant. In 1985, he and his wife Patricia Tudor Sandahl, founded Sandahl Partners, a consulting company specializing in organizational psychology which continues to flourish with a new generation of owners. For the past 25 years, as a full-time researcher, Christer has studied group- and organizational psychology and its implications for leadership and team development. He initiated and led the research group Leadership, Evaluation and Organizational Development (LEAD) at the Medical Management Centre, Karolinska Institutet. In addition, he is a member of the Royal Swedish Academy of Engineering Sciences.

Mia von Knorring is Psychologist, and Associate Professor in Healthcare Organization at Karolinska Institutet, Stockholm and has a background in journalism. For more than 20 years she has taught managerial leadership at post-graduate level and has been counselling managers on leadership. Her research focus is on professionalism in the managerial role. Currently, she leads the research group Leadership in Healthcare and Academia at the Department of Learning, Informatics, Management and Ethics (LIME), Karolinska Institutet. In 2014 she was awarded the distinction "Leadership promotor of the year" by the Swedish Leadership Academy in Healthcare for her strong commitment to the promotion of research-oriented leadership development.

Introduction

1

Managers wrestle daily with emotionally fraught issues. Because emotions and relationships influence organizational energy, commitment, and financial results, these issues are naturally of managerial concern. They are far too important to ignore. Emotions can appear as irrational expressions of human feelings causing trouble for managers as well as for their co-workers. However, emotions can also be a valuable source of information for professional judgment and decision-making. Dealing with emotionally challenging situations in a professional way is therefore one of the most important managerial responsibilities. The manager is ultimately responsible for the conditions that create a compassionate and effective work environment, where feelings can be expressed in constructive ways that benefit the entire organization.

When the book was first published in Swedish 10 years ago, there were few scientific studies on leadership and emotions, and surprisingly little research was available on the special conditions of the managerial position in relation to reason and emotions. Today, this is a rapidly growing field of research.

In this first English edition, updated with recent research in the field, we explore various aspects of managerial professionalism from this perspective. How do emotions and relationships influence organizational energy, commitment, and outcomes in terms of organizational efficiency? In what way can emotions contribute to judicious and wise decisions? When should managers reveal their feelings? When should they suppress them? How should they deal with other people's emotional expressions using both feeling and reason? How can they deal with employees' emotions in a way that contributes to a healthy and constructive work environment? What distinguishes leadership in a managerial role from leadership in other roles and what is unique for managers?

As authors of this book, we are active in several areas related to leadership: group and organizational psychology, management, governance, and organizational development. We have conducted research from various perspectives on the role and responsibility of managers, and we have both held managerial positions. We have

C. Sandahl, M. von Knorring, *Managing with Sense and Sensitivity*,
https://doi.org/10.1007/978-3-031-24109-3_1

extensive experience of management supervision and consultation within various organizations, public and private. The book is based on our experience and research. We present knowledge that is essential for leaders on all levels, from CEOs to front-line managers, in different fields of business, in public, and in nongovernmental organizations. It is a book for managers, for those who expect to become managers, and for those who have a professional interest in managerial leadership.

The Swedish edition of the forerunner of this book [*Chef med känsla och förnuft*] has enjoyed wide success. It is currently used as a standard text for managers at several organizations and is required reading at several universities and other institutes of higher education where leadership issues are in focus. We wish to thank to Erica Falkenström who was the co-author of the Swedish editions.

The aim of this book, as in all previous editions, remains the same: to support managers in their efforts to strike a balance between feeling and reason in a professional manner. It is our hope that the book can contribute both theoretically and practically to the ongoing discussions on leadership among managers, researchers, students, and employees.

Managers must develop their own ways of being a leader based on who they are as persons, their convictions, and the circumstances in which they find themselves. There are no ready-made recipes, instructions, or behaviours that suit all. The only tools that are at hand are judgment, experience, reflection, and general knowledge. This book provides the latter in the hope that it will inspire readers to reflect on their own experience and develop their personal skills as leaders.

The Book: An Overview

The following is a short overview of the nine chapters of the book.

Emotional Challenges In Chap. 2, we describe the fundamental emotional challenges faced by managers. The power to make decisions and take initiatives that come with the role is discussed in relation to the simultaneous dependence on the reactions of the co-workers, which can neither be controlled nor predicted. The relationship between managerial leadership, emotions, and organizational performance is also discussed. The chapter concludes by placing reliability, predictability, and fairness at the core of the manager role.

Leadership, Power, and Authority In Chap. 3, we give an overview and synthesis of the leadership field, including a description of theories of charisma, personality, leadership style, situational, transformational, and shared leadership. Similarities and differences between the concepts of power and authority are explored, a theme which is further developed in Chaps. 7 and 8.

Emotions in the Workplace In Chap. 4, the meaning of affects, emotions, and feelings, including the survival value of affects and bonds between people in human evolution, is described. Current research on the relationship between emotions and work is presented. The biological basis of emotions and the primary affects are explained, as well as the concepts of emotional intelligence and emotional contagion. The use of emotions as information and an essential precondition to reflection and wise decision-making is introduced.

Why Do We Want to Work? Chapter 5 addresses the meaning of work and the forces that motivates people to work. Why do we want to work at all? Needs-based human motivation and the biological basis for motivation and how these forces can impact the work environment and the organization are described. We also give some recommendations regarding organizational prerequisites for human motivation, development, and wellness.

Group Dynamics In Chap. 6, we describe various aspects of dynamic processes within teams and work groups. We discuss why managers need to understand the dynamics of emotions and reason in group interaction and how they themselves influence (and are influenced by) these dynamics. Reference is made to the concept of trust and the importance of psychological safety for team effectiveness and organizational results. Group development is described and how managerial leadership must adjust to the needs of the group in the different developmental stages.

Leading as a Manager Chapter 7 involves a closer look at the manager's everyday work life and how managerial leadership influences productivity, quality of work, and employee well-being. A tool for analyzing managerial leadership tasks is introduced. The purpose of the "managerial leadership grid" (MLG) is to provide a system for the exploration of managerial practical challenges such as those encountered in employee interactions, work delegation, and demands for change and development in the context of group dynamics and authentic and transformational leadership ideals.

How to Act Professionally in the Manager Role In Chap. 8, we describe and analyze the concept of role. Focus is on what professionalism in a managerial role can entail. A model is presented that can help managers to take their role in a professional way and can serve as a guide to balance reason and emotions at work, without losing sight of personal ethics and the organizations overall purpose.

Developing as a Manager with Sense and Sensitivity In Chap. 9, we emphasize the importance of learning from experience through reflection and how it can contribute to the development of self-confidence and self-esteem as a manager. The need to create time and space for reflection is underscored, and models for managerial supervision and learning are briefly described.

Emotional Challenges in Leadership 2

The courage to doubt.

In this chapter, we describe the emotional leadership challenges that managers face. These challenges include, among other things, the manager's dependence on the co-workers, the manager's vulnerability associated with high visibility in a direct sense and in an indirect sense, and the loneliness of managerial work. The way in which managers cope with their challenges influences their leadership style and, ultimately, their success as managers

As a manager, you are often faced with emotionally demanding situations. For example, tense situations may arise in meetings you lead. Suddenly, something unexpected happens – perhaps someone introduces a sensitive issue that you are not prepared for, or someone makes a personal attack against another, or others reveal criticisms of your managerial actions or style that may even have been secretly planned. Or the classic after-meeting response: Following a calm meeting in which members seemed in agreement, you immediately after the meeting observe tense, even heated, conversations among the members. You have no idea what is going on.

All managers face challenges when their judgment, social skills, or motivations are tested. You may think you handled a situation or crisis poorly. You may become aware that others share this opinion. These are painful insights for any manager. Yet managers who do not engage in self-criticism or who blind themselves to others' criticisms are likely to continue their suboptimal behavior.

Much of the managerial literature describes managers as individuals with significant responsibility for the future of their organizations and the well-being of their co-workers. Our business culture assumes that managers are in control: they have the answer to every question. But is that possible – or even desirable?

We have found, contrary to this common perception of the managerial role, that the managers we have worked with over the years often say they lack full control. Frequently, they argue that they cannot exert their influence in ways they would like. Instead, they describe a managerial role that is often characterized by extreme pressure and incompatible demands from people at both upper and lower organizational

C. Sandahl, M. von Knorring, *Managing with Sense and Sensitivity*, https://doi.org/10.1007/978-3-031-24109-3_2

levels as well as from people outside the organization. We have heard managers describe emotional situations – outside their control – that they do not know how to influence or control as events unfold. And we have met top-level managers, CEOs, chairpersons of boards, and others who argue that they are victims of sudden market fluctuations, political decisions, competitors' drastic strategy changes, unions' demands, and subordinate managers who are ill informed, obstructionist, etcetera. Daily events seem to govern managers to a greater degree than is usually thought. Intentions and long-term strategies have less importance than we may want to believe (Holmberg & Tyrstrup, 2010; Weick, 1995).

However, is this description of the powerless managerial role completely accurate? We think not. As a manager, you have influence, in varying degrees. To deny the scope and power of your influence is to deny the reality and responsibility of your position. A manager can exert influence over the organization and its co-workers in ways that have both short- and long-term consequences. Of course, your power to exercise your influence is in part dependent on your place in the organization's hierarchy. As managers rise in the hierarchy, their actions and decisions obviously become more influential and have long-lasting effects (Jaques, 1996; Jones, 2012). With these actions and decisions, managers can also create an organizational culture that reflects their own values and interests. Through their ideas and mental models, they can influence both the understanding of what needs to be done and the development of mental models among middle managers, who in turn become links to lower hierarchical levels in the organization. If they act as trustworthy role models and thereby gain authority, their capacity to affect the organization is considerable (Larsson et al., 2005).

Nevertheless, we admit to the partial truth of managers' lived experience of dependence and powerlessness. How can we explain this paradox? Managers can, among other things, promote an organizational vision, set goals, control resources, and plan projects and activities. They can also legitimize certain actions and not others as they make decisions and take initiatives that affect many people, inside and outside the organization.

What they cannot do, however, is to be certain in their predictions and control how others will respond to their decisions and initiatives. A well-intentioned and well thought out decision that affects many co-workers may, for example, be met with suspicion or even hostility. Consider an example at the individual level.

> A manager who wants to reward a co-worker for her good work offers her advancement in the organization. The manager expects the co-worker will react positively and appreciatively; however, to the manager's amazement, the co-worker reacted negatively. Tears come into her eyes, and she asks for permission to leave the meeting. Further investigation reveals the co-worker felt safe and competent in her current position and had no wish to take on new challenges.

There is always some measure of surprise and uncertainty in human responses (Stacey & Mowles, 2016). Given this reality, one can understand why some managers say they have little influence over their co-workers and other organizational stakeholders. Complicated feelings often are involved in such highly sensitive work situations.

The Relationship Among Managerial Leadership, Emotions, and Organizational Performance

It is often assumed that the manager's way of being and exercising leadership is of immense importance for the organization. Modern leadership research, however, complicates this conclusion. Only a few research studies have found a straightforward connection between how managers lead and how their organizations perform. Stordeur et al.'s (2001) study revealed, for example, that slightly less than a tenth of organizational results are attributable to managerial leadership. It is not surprising to conclude that profitability or other measures of organizational results depend on several interacting factors and not just on managerial leadership (Alvesson, 2016; Jackson & Parry, 2008; Northouse, 2007; Yukl, 2013). These factors may include market conditions, competition, staff composition, salary structure, and corporate culture. At the same time, if managerial leadership influences even 10% of organizational results, we may conclude that such leadership is a significantly influential economic factor.

Group level research supports these conclusions. At the same time, one must be aware that there is a large variation among the positive and negative "outliers." Case studies show that certain individuals with strong convictions or clear visions can, under favorable circumstances, exert a decisive influence on the development of the organization (Collins, 2001; Zaccaro et al., 2018).

However, because leadership is a complex subject, it is difficult to identify straightforward, simple connections between the actions of managers, emotional work climates, and organizational performance. Nevertheless, certain indications suggest strong, indirect connections do exist. Our keyword search using "emotion" and "leadership" resulted in almost 600 articles in a leading journal, *Leadership Quarterly*. Of these articles, about 90% were published after the year 2000, with a majority published in the last decade. We will explore this theme further in Chap. 3. However, we present a few examples from this research here.

What Does Research Say?

After the millennium shift, researchers have shown an increasing interest in leaders' emotional displays and followers' outcomes as well as leaders' and followers' regulation of emotions. Several studies claim a connection exists between organizational performance and the manager's ability to handle the work group's emotions. For example, Gooty et al. (2010), in an article that summarized the results of current research on the relationship between leadership and emotions, described the increasing interest in emotions and leadership as an "affective revolution." In fact, a noticeable shift in this research has occurred: from a narrow focus on cognition and behavior to a broader focus on how emotions affect thinking and behavior. Empirical support is now found in the literature for the importance of emotions in the relationships between managers and co-workers as well as for the linkage between emotional states and the work environment. We explore this change in focus in the following examples.

Researchers have examined how managers' ways of being affect co-workers emotionally, and vice versa. Schneider (2014) found that passive co-workers evoke more negative emotions than active co-workers. The latter group tends to evoke satisfaction, joy, gratitude, and serenity in managers. This study illustrates how co-workers in a certain sense contribute to managers' exercise of leadership. The co-workers in the study likely were unaware of this response, had no intention of evoking this response, and had no idea that passive or active behavior could evoke different responses. Yet, as we all know, humans are always influenced by others. We know this from other contexts (e.g., family or school) even though we may not realize it is also true at work.

Ashkanasy and Humphrey (2011) argue that emotions within and between people affect emotional states in work groups and teams. This effect creates an emotional climate throughout the organization, which in turn influences organizational performance. When team members are, for example, frustrated, angry, sad, satisfied, or happy, these emotions affect other team members and even the mood of the entire team. If the situation continues, other teams that are dependent on or cooperate with the original team may be similarly affected. Ashkanasy and Humphrey claim empirical support exists for the fact that emotions in individuals and groups at different levels within an organization affect their interaction. However, it is not yet known how changes in co-workers' emotional states can affect overall organizational performance.

McColl-Kennedy and Anderson (2002) studied how managers' transformational leadership influences co-workers' performance in terms of frustration or optimism. The negative influence of frustration on co-worker performance was larger than the positive influence of optimism on co-worker performance. This research suggests that the inability of an organization to manage the emotion of frustration among co-workers can damage not only co-workers but also the organization itself.

Skogstad et al. (2014) reached a similar conclusion in a Norwegian study, although they did not link negative emotions to the results of operations. These researchers examined the relative effect of constructive leadership, laissez-faire leadership, and tyrannical leadership on co-worker job satisfaction. They found that the destructive forms of leadership had better predictability than the constructive forms. The destructive leaders exerted more negative influence on the organization than the positive influence exerted by the constructive leaders. The study supports the principle that "bad is stronger than good."

In another Norwegian study, Glasø and Einarsen (2006, 2008) found that negative emotions such as disappointment, insecurity, and annoyance are often suppressed in the workplace while positive emotions such as enthusiasm, interest, and calmness are expressed or "faked." They identified this behavior more among managers than among co-workers. They also found that suppressing or faking emotions can create negative relationships between co-workers and managers, as well as influencing job satisfaction and health negatively in both groups. While they concluded that more constructive ways of dealing with emotions at work seem advisable, they offered no clear ideas or recommendations.

Ethical and Moral Challenges

Both co-workers and managers have a responsibility for how they affect each other. There are ethical and moral dimensions in everything we do – from everyday interactions to large, comprehensive business decisions. In most cases, it is quite easy to act ethically and morally when we distinguish between right and wrong. In addition, most people feel positive in some sense when they act ethically and morally. Such actions give us inner satisfaction and a deeper sense of meaning.

However, under certain circumstances, everyone's moral judgment can be tested. That includes managers especially if their self-interests are threatened or in situations when strong feelings are aroused. Then, the risk is that the lines between right and wrong are less clear. Perhaps, without much reflection, managers may then try to arrange reality best suited to their own interests. When personal privileges, promotions, or even friendships are at stake, people's moral judgment may cloud when making difficult decisions that involve compromise, betrayal, and selfishness.

On the other hand, personal convictions, and values – such as the benefits derived from the creation of a collaborative work climate or from the achievement of desired work results – give managers the foundation for what they wish to accomplish. It is quite clear, however, that these convictions and values can provoke difficult work conflicts, some of which are the result of co-workers' emotional responses.

Anxiety and fear among co-workers may be provoked, for example, when managers make decisions that co-workers suspect will lead to deteriorating work conditions. Some co-workers may experience debilitating stress; others may resign. If the responses are serious enough, managers must examine the situation, taking into consideration the effects of confirming, moderating, or reversing previous decisions. Such an examination can be particularly difficult if the decisions have had negative consequences for some co-workers. "What if the company's most productive co-workers quit!?" "What if a co-worker who is already experiencing stress nears a breakdown?"

Contemplation of such outcomes are undoubtedly emotionally challenging for managers. They are also ethically complicated when emotions prevail over reason. Actions taken too hastily may be regretted later. For example, even when managers' anger at a co-worker is justified by that co-worker's moral transgression, responsible managers think about the possible outcomes of expressing their anger directly and clearly. The managers' response may decrease other co-workers' trust in their leadership if they are too harsh. Or this trust may increase if co-workers observe that their managers have acted with integrity (Shao, 2019). It is a tricky balance. Therefore, managers are well-advised to think carefully before they act in sensitive co-worker situations. Managers, like everyone else, have the opportunity, as well as the responsibility, to understand the origin of their feelings. One needs to understand the issues behind the emotions aroused and discuss them openly. Such an approach usually creates respect, trust, and confidence in those involved – and lead, not least, to inner satisfaction and pride in having done the best one could.

Three Emotional Challenges

As a manager, you often take joy and satisfaction in the work, but sometimes you experience frustration, disappointment, anger, or sadness. Perhaps unsatisfactory co-worker performance or inadequate upper management support explain these negative emotions. While you may think it is inappropriate to show these emotions openly, falsification or suppression of such emotions, as Glasø and Einarsen (2006, 2008) warn, can be harmful. Yet, at the same time, managers must exercise caution so that they do not overwhelm or distract co-workers with angry outbursts or critical remarks. A balance is required.

Next, we will describe three emotional challenges that we find integral to the managerial role. These challenges include the manager's dependence on the co-worker, the manager's vulnerability associated with high visibility in a direct sense and in an indirect sense, and the loneliness of managerial work. The way in which managers cope with these challenges influences their leadership style and, ultimately, their success as managers.

Dependence

Even though managers have power, as described above, they are also familiar with the challenge posed by their own dependence on others. They depend on their co-workers, other managers, and internal structures. They are also constrained by laws and regulations, financial limitations, and political forces. A paradox that many managers tend to ignore is that they are accountable for the outcomes of collaborative work in which they may have only the illusion of control (Grint, 2005; Stacey & Mowles, 2016). Co-workers who manage their work in ways they find appropriate and meaningful often have a great deal of control. They decide whom to trust and whose authority they will accept. Managers are well-advised to understand they govern by the consent of the governed. Managers who have so much hubris that they never doubt their decisions risk being seen by co-workers as stubborn and arrogant.

Unfortunately, we find managers often shirk responsibility for the negative outcomes of the group's collaborative work. We observe that managers are generally expected to choose a co-worker as a scapegoat to take the blame when problems occur. Such scapegoating undermines co-workers' trust in managers and in organizations.

Visibility

Another challenge concerns the high visibility that is associated with the managerial position. The challenge posed by such visibility is its close association with vulnerability. Probably every manager has felt vulnerable at work at some point. Managers are expected to take control as needed, but only then. Co-workers, however, often disagree with managers on when (and how much) managerial control is necessary.

One person's ugly authoritarianism may be another person's insightful leadership. Inevitably, managers (figuratively and often actually) stand before their co-workers. They are visible to everyone as "the boss." Everyone's eyes are on the manager.

The co-worker role has less visibility and therefore, in some sense, less vulnerability than the manager role. As group members, co-workers often decide for themselves whether to speak in a meeting or otherwise to take the initiative on some issue. Co-workers often have the luxury of remaining silent or of avoiding responsibility. At the same time, co-workers can complain, openly or secretly, about their managers and organizations.

Managers do not have this luxury or freedom. Exercising leadership means stepping forward and taking responsibility in critical situations and thinking about the consequences of actions, including the consequences for co-workers. Most people find it hard to criticize other people because they have experienced the pain and humiliation of being on the receiving end of criticism. Managers' criticisms of co-worker performance can result in a variety of negative responses from co-workers: anger, resentment, and demotivation, for example. Such performance reviews are difficult to deliver for managers. Sometimes it happens that the performance review is so gently delivered that co-workers miss the point. Are they being praised or criticized? Mixed messages are confusing. Striking the right balance between clarity and compassion in performance reviews, where both managers' and co-workers' self-esteem are at stake is tricky. However, it is a task that the visible manager cannot avoid.

However, many managers enjoy their visibility. This is a resource, but if the manager is too dependent on being in the limelight, it is problematic. Destructive leadership, of which pathological narcissism is an example, will be described in Chaps. 3 and 7. When things go well, many of us like being the center of attention, basking in the admiration of co-workers, other stakeholders, and the public. But things do not always go well; they may even go badly. In such moments, managers, like everyone else, need honest feedback and support. Unfortunately, such feedback and support are not always forthcoming because of the ambivalence many individuals feel about people in positions of power. Managers must find other ways to maintain and strengthen their self-confidence when faced with such adversity (see Chap. 9).

Given the tension and stress associated with managerial visibility, managers may be tempted to hide as they seek some anonymity among their co-workers. Giving into this temptation risks abdication of responsibility. Admittedly, it is sometimes appropriate to pass the leadership reins temporarily to someone else. The decisive factor is whether the managerial motive is avoidance of responsibility or recognition that others are more suited for the task at hand.

Loneliness

Most managers are familiar with the emotional challenge of the loneliness inherent in their leadership role. Identifying and assigning tasks are rarely the most problematic managerial tasks. The difficulty lies in managing the co-worker-manager emotions that surface in the execution of those tasks. How should managers handle their disappointment and anger when a co-worker has not taken responsibility for an important task? How should managers respond to their own managers' criticism of and dissatisfaction with the performance of the operation they supervise? How should managers deal with their own emotions when they present what they imagine to be a very good idea, and the co-workers respond with silence?

Managers generally face these questions on their own. In situations involving strong feelings, they can hardly consult the co-workers they supervise, and many hesitate to consult senior managers with a fear that it might hit back in the salary review. In a trusting relationship with a superior manager, such challenges can of course be ventilated, and one can expect to get constructive help. Another possibility is to seek support from one's management team. However, there is rarely opportunity to talk through managers' everyday problems and insecurity sufficiently to fully solve emotional issues. In Chap. 9, we return to how support for managers can be designed.

The Core of Managerial Leadership

These three challenges – dependence, visibility, and loneliness – are emotionally fraught. It is the human condition to experience disappointment, grief, anger, shame, and many other negative emotions. Fortunately, we also experience joy, satisfaction, pride, and other positive emotions when things are going well.

We think the core of managerial leadership is about dealing responsibly with the emotions experienced at work. Thus, dependence, visibility that evokes vulnerability, and loneliness are unavoidable in the managerial role. Managing requires knowing yourself, analyzing your motives, and using empathy and intuition. Managing involves knowing when to act and when to refrain from action (Badaracco, 2006). According to Denhardt and Denhardt (2006), people need to follow the rhythm of human interaction using sensitivity, intuition, and timing. When is it appropriate to act? How should one act? When should one stop? These are questions best answered using emotions and reason.

The Courage to Doubt

When managers have resolved an emotionally challenging situation, they usually feel competent and confident. But there are also situations when managers have doubts about how they handled (or will handle) certain situations. They begin to question their managerial competence. In such crises of self-doubt, many managers conclude it may be best to set aside uncertainties and hesitations. Doubt should be kept at a proper distance as they act confidently with conviction. In some organizations, it might even be the norm to have such an attitude.

Deciding to act with conviction, ignoring doubts, however, may involve contradictions. Rollo May, the American philosopher, psychologist, and psychotherapist, describes the act of resolving the tense relationship between doubt and conviction as the highest form of courage (May, 1994). Doubt, which implies openness and responsiveness in decision-making, has validity (Kahneman, 2011). Doubt does not block thinking in the way that persistent stubbornness and single-mindedness do. From this perspective, doubt, as ambivalence, has almost a moral quality. One can rightly be wary of managers who never have doubts. May writes that we long for leaders like Abraham Lincoln who openly acknowledged his doubts and yet just as openly maintained his commitment (May, 1994). Commitment and conviction are thus healthiest when they exist despite natural doubts.

Self-doubt is a natural emotion from time to time for many managers, especially when certain tasks seem to challenge their ability to handle them. According to Elliott Jaques (1996), an authority in the field of organizational psychology and leadership, the problem is that solving the dilemmas and uncertainties inherent in the managerial role can sometimes be too demanding. Jaques thinks limits exist, in varying degrees, to the amount of complexity people can manage. For most of us, when we reach the limits of our ability to understand and manage complexity, we no longer discover the inherent conflicts that exist in complex situations. The risk at this point is that we will act as if dilemmas and uncertainties do not exist. Then, we only discover our error when it is too late to reverse course. Allowing oneself to doubt stimulates reflection and careful analysis of the situation, thus avoiding mistakes.

The Need for Self-Reflection

As this chapter emphasizes, we think leadership is more about emotions and human relationships than managers generally imagine. Therefore, we conclude that several similarities exist between the role of the manager and the role of the psychotherapist. The goals and structures of these two roles are, of course, completely different. However, both roles deal with the processes and dynamics of emotions and human relationships. Psychotherapists spend considerable time and effort thinking about themselves and others: what is said, what is done, what is meant, and how is this best handled to pursue the task at hand. They often need to exchange ideas and experiences with others in the same role. Not least, of necessity, sometimes they must be satisfied with the imperfect when decisions and actions are disappointing in their resolution. Just because we might find some similarities between the emotional work involved in psychotherapy and management, it does not mean that we underestimate the differences. In the psychotherapy, the client always has the final word regarding the goals and the pace of the therapy. Managerial leadership on the other hand requires an emotional commitment to goals and purpose on a level that the psychotherapist cannot take.

In an oft-cited article, Sigmund Freud, the father of psychoanalysis, once described three occupations as "impossible" (Freud, 1937). Freud described the psychoanalyst, the educator, and the politician as professionals whose outcomes are necessarily unsatisfactory. Although Freud did not include managers in this group, we think his description of the "impossible" occupation is equally applicable to the managerial role. Because the managerial role involves interpersonal relationships, conflicts, and authority and communication issues, the work of managers is complex and emotionally challenging. To be credible as well as effective, managers must be their own tools for self-examination. They must learn who they are and how they make decisions.

This is not an original insight. The philosopher and theologian, Thomas Aquinas, argued as early as the thirteenth century that "action follows being" (*agere sequitur esse*). Another historic role model is the Roman emperor Marcus Aurelius (121–180), who reflected in his *Meditations* on how to become more virtuous, more just, and more resistant to temptation. If managers, like Marcus Aurelius, strive to find a fixed inner point, a core to rely on, their work will be easier, both for themselves and for their co-workers.

On a smaller, and less heroic, scale, this same intention was demonstrated by a group of Swedish first-line nurse managers and their co-workers. Their work strategy was to develop virtues aimed at achieving the goals of nursing and establishing a work climate that motivated staff and improved performance. As reported by Johansson et al. (2010), this was the central aim of their professional work. Using self-reflection, managers can achieve such an inner point that acts as a "being" to fall back on. As people's credibility increases, their vulnerability reduces, and they become more predictable. While no shortcuts or patented solutions to achieving this state exist, the mere recognition that emotional challenges are part of everyday work life for managers is a useful point of departure. It is essential that managers become aware of others' emotions as well as their own emotions.

When managers succeed in acquiring a more nuanced understanding of their own and others' emotions, they have travelled a long way toward managing with sense and sensitivity. When their actions are based in their moral convictions and when they know themselves and where they are headed, they can feel secure in their role. However, perfection in the managerial role, as in life, is far from achievable, but managing fairly, predictably, and reliably is possible. That is the message of this book.

References

Alvesson, M. (2016). *Reflexive leadership. Organizing in an imperfect world.* Sage.

Ashkanasy, N. M., & Humphrey, R. H. (2011). Current emotion research in organizational behavior. *Emotion Review, 3*(2), 214–224.

Badaracco, J. L. (2006). *Questions of character. Illuminating the heart of leadership through literature.* Harvard Business School Press.

Collins, J. (2001). *Good to great: Why some companies make the leap … and others don't.* Harper Business.

Denhardt, R. B., & Denhardt, J. V. (2006). The dance of leadership: The art of leading in business, government, and society. ME Sharpe.

Freud, S. (1937). Analysis terminable and interminable. *International Journal of Psychoanalysis, 18*, 373–405.

Glasø, L., & Einarsen, S. (2006). Experienced affects in leader–subordinate relationships. *Scandinavian Journal of Management,* 22(1), 49–73.

Glasø, L., & Einarsen, S. (2008). Emotion regulation in leader follower relationships. *European Journal of Work and Organizational Psychology, 17*(4), 482–500.

Gooty, J., Connelly, S., Griffith, J., & Gupta, A. (2010). Leadership, affect and emotions: A state of the science review. *The Leadership Quarterly, 21*(6), 979–1004.

Grint, K. (2005). *Leadership: Limits and possibilities*. Palgrave.

Holmberg, I., & Tyrstrup, M. (2010). Well then – What now? An everyday approach to managerial leadership. *Leadership, 6*(4), 353–372. https://doi.org/10.1177/1742715010379306

Jackson, B., & Parry, K. (2008). *A very short, fairly interesting and reasonably cheap book about studying leadership*. Sage.

Jaques, E. (1996). *Requisite organization. A total system for effective managerial organization and managerial leadership for the 21st century*. Cason Hall.

Johansson, G., Andersson, L., & Sandahl, C. (2010). Between being and doing – The nature of leadership of first-line nurse managers and registered nurses. *The Journal of Clinical Nursing, 19*, 2619–2628.

Jones, G. R. (2012). *Organizational theory, design, and change: Global edition*. Pearson Education.

Kahneman, D. (2011). *Thinking, fast and slow*. Farrar, Straus and Giroux.

Larsson, G., Sjöberg, M., Vrbanjac, A., & Björkman, T. (2005). Indirect leadership in a military context: A qualitative study on how to do it. *Leadership and Organization Development Journal, 26*(3), 215–227.

May, R. (1994). *The courage to create*. WW Norton & Co.

McColl-Kennedy, J. R., & Anderson, R. D. (2002). Impact of leadership style and emotions on subordinate performance. *The Leadership Quarterly, 13*, 545–559.

Northouse, P. G. (2007). *Leadership: Theory and practice* (4th ed.). Sage.

Reed, B. D., & Bazalgette, J. L. (2006). Organisational role analysis at the Grubb Institute of Behavioural studies: Origins and development. In J. Newton, S. Long, & B. Sievers (Eds.), *Coaching in depth: The organisational role analysis approach*. Karnac.

Schneider, A. (2014). Emotional responses of leaders to passive versus active members. *Leadership, 10*(4), 412–436.

Shao, B. (2019). Moral anger as a dilemma? An investigation on how leader moral anger influences follower trust. *The Leadership Quarterly, 30*(3), 365–382.

Skogstad, A., Aasland, M. S., Nielsen, M. B., Hetland, J., Matthiesen, S. B., & Einarsen, S. (2014). The relative effects of constructive, laissez-faire, and tyrannical leadership on subordinate job satisfaction: Results from two prospective and representative studies. *Zeitschrift für Psychologie, 222*(4), 221–232.

Stacey, R. D., & Mowles, C. (2016). *Strategic management and organizational dynamics. The challenge of complexity to ways of thinking about organizations*. Pearson.

Stordeur, S., D'Hoore, W., & Vandenberghe, C. (2001). Leadership, organizational stress, and emotional exhaustion among hospital nursing staff. *Journal of Advanced Nursing, 35*, 533–542.

Weick, K. (1995). *Sensemaking in organizations*. Sage.

Yukl, G. (2013). *Leadership in organizations* (8th ed.). Pearson.

Zaccaro, S. J., Green, J. P., Dubrow, S., & Kolze, M. (2018). Leader individual differences, situational parameters, and leadership outcomes: A comprehensive review and integration. *The Leadership Quarterly, 29*(1), 2–43.

Leadership, Power, and Authority

3

Acting with authority or exercising authoritarian power.

Managerial leadership is not an agreed-upon concept. We begin by problematizing definitions of leadership. We continue by describing various leadership theories presented in the literature and then discuss the difference between power and authority

The American organizational psychologist, Gary Yukl, defined leadership as "the process of influencing others to understand and agree about what needs to be done and how to do it, and the process of facilitating individual and collective efforts to accomplish shared objectives" (Yukl, 2013, p. 23). While this definition reflects a commonly held view of leadership, it has its critics. For example, Yukl's definition has been criticized for its one-sided focus on the "leader" that downplays the leader's interaction with and dependence on "followers." Others have argued that Yukl's definition implicitly assumes that only leaders in formal leadership positions can exercise leadership, even though most of us have been in situations where co-workers or "followers" have taken the lead. A more general criticism of this leadership definition assumes that leadership can be observed by others when in fact a large part of leadership is unobservable. As Badaracco (2002) points out, we cannot observe what takes place in a leader's mind when, for example, the leader decides not to act.

It is sometimes said that as many leadership definitions can be found, so as the number of people who have tried to define leadership. Indeed, the leadership descriptive commentary is extensive (Jackson & Parry, 2008). Dinh et al. (2014), for example, identified more than 60 different leadership theories. Nevertheless, many leadership researchers claim we still do not really understand leadership (Avolio et al., 2012; Crevani et al., 2010; George, 2000; Grint, 1997). In an article, Alvesson and Sveningsson (2003) even challenged the significance of the leadership concept and argued that leadership is such an elusive phenomenon that we need to question its relevance.

C. Sandahl, M. von Knorring, *Managing with Sense and Sensitivity*, https://doi.org/10.1007/978-3-031-24109-3_3

In the leadership literature, "leader" and "follower" are often paired. We think this leader-follower pairing, in which leadership is prioritized over followership, diminishes the idea that leadership is a collaborative process. The tendency to attribute unique qualities to the leader has been described as "the romance of leadership" (Meindl et al., 1985; Meindl, 1995). This romantic notion supports the myth that individual leaders are the most important contributors to organizational success (Alvesson, 2017).

A common way of examining the leadership role is to look at the leader's everyday interactions with co-workers. These interactions present evidence of the leader's ability (or inability) to identify the actions required in various situations that will facilitate the conditions leading to their accomplishment. In this examination, leadership is about timing, sensitivity, and relationships (Badaracco, 2002). Viewing leadership as such a context-dependent and elusive phenomenon means, we are unlikely to find simple leadership recipes. Each situation requires analysis in its specific context. Depending on the external factors, on the temporary composition or mood of the group, and/or on the actions of individual co-workers, leaders perform their leadership role differently at different times.

Thus, contrary to the view that leadership is almost wholly defined by the leader's expression and promotion of visions and goals, we maintain that leadership is also defined by the leader's everyday actions, initiatives, and decisions aimed at achieving those visions and goals. In fact, leadership may sometimes mean taking no action and allowing the passage of time to resolve situations. In such circumstances, probably only the leaders realize they have exercised leadership; they know their inaction and silence achieved a desired conclusion (Badaracco, 2002).

In this chapter (and book), we describe leadership as part of, and integrated with, daily managerial work. We focus on leadership performed by managers and formal leaders, regardless of organizational level.

Leadership Theories

While we do not intend to present various leadership theories in detail, we still need to present a brief summary of how leadership theories have changed throughout history – or rather changed and not changed. Admittedly, several new leadership theories have been introduced since the emergence of the managerial leadership role with the advent of the Industrial Age. These theories have created new ways of looking at leadership in parallel with new economic and social ideas. Yet, at the same time, earlier theories have survived and developed. As Northouse (2007) observes, the view of leadership has followed several parallel tracks.

Theories of Great Men, Charisma, and Personality

A popular idea, which originally arose in Great Britain during the nineteenth century, was that good leadership derives from the natural qualities of divinely gifted individuals. This idea, which was labeled the great man theory, is primarily attributed to the Scottish philosopher and historian Thomas Carlyle (1795–1891), who lectured on heroes and their role in shaping history. Although Carlyle was disappointed in the teachings of the Church, he still maintained that God sends great men as saviors of the world. Scholars have since noted the authoritarian implications of Carlyle's ideas.

Although few leadership commentators today claim that God chooses great men as leaders, the idea of the strong male leader persists. Powerful charismatic political leaders, some of whom have almost a cult-like appeal, lead some nations today; some citizens view these leaders as saviors, while others view them as threats. Much speculation exists on how these strong men come to power and on the influences that shape their authoritarian personalities. Are these men the result of people's desire for security and safety? Are they the leaders of populist movements that arise when liberal democracies cannot provide citizens with financial equality and equal justice? Is the explanation, as Freud thought, that people have a deep-seated need for a powerful father figure (Spector, 2016)? Whatever the reason, Carlyle's theory still has a strong attraction for some people. It is a theory worth thinking about, especially in times of totalitarian threats to civil society and democratic governments.

About 100 years later, theories of charismatic leadership were again promoted in the 1980s by management consultants and some researchers (Bass, 1990). In some sense, the theory of charismatic leadership was a revival of the great man theory. Although the popularity of charismatic leadership had gradually diminished by the 1990s and early 2000s, as the new century progressed, charismatic and autocratic political leaders in some countries emerged. Leadership research began to reflect renewed interest in this phenomenon. Since 2017, we have seen an increasing number of scientific publications on charismatic leadership with titles such as "Playing the trump card: Why we select overconfident leaders and why it matters" (Ronay et al., 2019).

Research on the link between personality traits and leadership shows that successful leaders generally have less pretentious and more relatable personalities than well-known charismatic leaders (Woods & West, 2019). While charismatic leaders may be perceived as innovative, exceptional, and original, they may also be perceived as narcissistic, emotionally fragile, and lacking in self-esteem. Human resource personnel with recruitment experience admit it is easy to be misled by charismatic applicants who make a positive initial impression with their charm and enthusiasm. When hired, such people seem engaging and inspiring in customer meetings and at public appearances. However, in their day-to-day work, they may present quite a different leadership persona: they may be excessively demanding, unreasonably impatient, and dismissive of important details.

Despite the lack of research support for charisma as a success factor for leadership, there are of course exceptions. Many charismatic individuals have become successful leaders. (Steve Jobs, the entrepreneur, founder, and CEO of Apple Inc., was such a leader.) Nevertheless, personal charisma is no guarantee of leadership success. As important in such exceptions, if not more, are the leader's other personality traits: energy, self-confidence, internal locus of control, emotional stability, integrity, socialized power, performance focus, and low need for confirmation (see below).

Research on Personality

One theme in leadership theory, somewhat consistent with the great man theory, focuses on unique leadership qualities in successful leaders (e.g., Koestenbaum, 2010; Maccoby, 1981). The assumption that a strong relationship exists between some personality traits and leadership effectiveness seems to make sense from the practitioner's perspective. After all, recruitment and selection of leaders are in part based on the assessment of personality traits.

However, researchers in this tradition have long struggled to establish a clear connection between personality traits and successful leadership. Success has been measured by *leader effectiveness* (e.g., influence, performance, promotion, and followers' job satisfaction) or by *leadership emergence* (e.g., followers' observations of leaders in group situations or followers' reports on leaders on group processes). For example, in a meta-analysis of personality and leadership, Judge et al. (2002) found correlations between the well-researched Big Five dimensions of personality (neuroticism, extraversion, openness, agreeableness, and conscientiousness) (Costa & McCrae, 1992) and leadership effectiveness and emergence. Neuroticism was negatively associated with leadership. This result indicated that personality measured according to the Big Five dimensions at the group level had a strong explanatory power. Researchers within this tradition have concluded that extraversion, conscientiousness, and emotional stability are the three factors most strongly related to effectiveness as a leader (Woods & West, 2019).

In another meta-analysis, Judge et al. (2004) also identified a moderate correlation between leadership and intelligence. Experience suggests that it is unusual that excellent results on cognitive aptitude tests are required in a manager. However, results below average are problematic but can sometimes be compensated by excellent relationship skills. The conclusion is that there is evidence for the combination of measures of personality and intelligence in the assessment of candidates for leadership positions. However, making predictions at the individual level is a complicated endeavor because other factors – not least unknown contextual factors – may have an influence.

In summary, there is no guarantee that an individual with positive results on the assessment of personality traits and individual abilities will succeed as a manager. Success often depends on other factors, such as the organizational culture or the manager's relationships with superiors and co-workers. Experience and research have shown that some managers who lack these, or some of these, characteristics and abilities nevertheless advance in their organizations, and some might even become successful as leaders. On the other hand, people with positive outcomes from personality assessment may find themselves in difficult and challenging situations, where the probability to succeed is very low. An example could be to have a subordinate position, under a superior manager who, although extremely task-oriented, lacks basic human relationship skills, is obsessed with self-aggrandizing projects, or is overly suspicious, aggressive, unreliable, false, controlling, passive, or insecure. These are behaviors and characteristics proven negatively related to leadership (Larsson et al., 2012; Yukl, 2013).

In the selection of managers, it is easier to predict failure than success, because there is a direct relationship between negative personality traits and problematic leadership when leaders are dismissed, transferred, forced into early retirement, or simple stagnate. Often such leaders lack emotional stability, integrity, and interpersonal skills. This lack is typically evidenced by their defensiveness and arrogance (Woods & West, 2019).

Although individuals with certain personality traits may likely succeed as leaders, there is obviously no guarantee of such success. A leader with positive personality traits may achieve success in one context, but not in another. Moreover, two leaders with completely different personalities may both succeed in the same endeavor (Yukl, 2013).

Building on Yukl's (2013) research, Woods and West (2019) summarized the leadership research that deals with the common personality traits of successful leaders. It is important to remember that many others, who not are leaders or who are not especially successful leaders, may also have these same traits. Woods and West found the following eight personality traits most frequently among successful leaders:

1. High energy and stress tolerance levels – Successful leaders can work sustainably for long time periods. They are less affected by conflicts and crises than others. Even in moments of crisis and conflict, they convey calm and confidence.
2. Self-confidence – Successful leaders are inclined to be optimistic and confident when faced with difficulties. They manage problems instead of avoiding them. However, overly self-confident leaders may take unnecessarily risky or poor decisions.
3. Internal locus of control – Successful leaders think they have more control over their plans and actions than external forces. They like to exert their influence by acting proactively. They assume they can involve others in their areas of interest.
4. Emotional maturity – Successful leaders are less prone to mood swings, moments of irritability, or sudden outbursts than most other people. They exhibit a positive and optimistic attitude to co-workers. They are aware of their strengths, weaknesses, and typical responses.
5. Personal integrity – Successful leaders are honest, open, and reliable. These traits are reflected in their actions. They do what they promise. They rarely act primarily from self-interest.
6. Socialized power motivation – Successful leaders want to achieve that which promotes the organization's interests and their co-workers' development. They are not motivated by personalized power needs (i.e., the need to promote self-interests).
7. Achievement orientation – Successful leaders are performance-oriented; however, a linear relationship does not exist between performance focus and performance outcome. A leader who is overly performance driven risks appearing egotistically ambitious to others.

8. Low need for affiliation – Successful leaders do not require others' confirmation (approval) of their performance. They do not need to be liked, although they still value others' good opinions of them.

Yukl (2013) and Woods and West (2019) emphasize the importance of managing the practical structures and processes of the organization. Therefore, the leader must be well acquainted with the organization and its context. They also emphasize the importance of the leader's conceptual ability. This is the ability to understand the work environment so that problems can be analyzed effectively without over-complication or oversimplification. It is crucial that leaders can simplify organizing, planning, and decision-making, which in turn increases confidence among co-workers.

In addition, Yukl (2013) and Woods and West (2019) stress the importance of leaders' ability to manage relationships with their co-workers. Leaders must be aware of their own emotional needs even as they respond to others' emotional needs.

Leadership Style Theories

Some leadership theories, as described above, highlight leaders' personality traits and abilities. Another leadership research stream focuses on leaders' ways of leading – their leadership style. This stream of research emerged in the early forties when the concepts of authoritarian, democratic, and laisse-faire leadership were introduced (Lewin et al., 1939). It has been concluded that *laissez-faire* leadership, in which leaders abdicate responsibility and avoid decision-making, has a very negative effect on an organization – on its culture, its performance, and co-worker health (Inceoglu et al., 2018; Larsson et al., 2018; Lewin et al., 1939; Nyberg, 2009).

This research stream also addresses theories related to task-oriented leadership and relationship-oriented leadership. For example, American surveys conducted in the 1950s showed that managers' leadership differed, depending on whether their focus was on creating good relationships with and between co-workers or on performing organizational tasks (Blake & Mouton, 1985). One conclusion from this research stream is that an either-or focus is not needed; the concern for people and the concern for results are obviously complementary.

This leadership discussion currently touches on other issues such as the challenges involved in leading change and the importance of maintaining external networks while representing the organization (Woods & West, 2019; Yukl, 2013).

Situational Leadership Theories

Another major leadership research stream, which originated in the 1960s, emphasizes the need for leaders to be sensitive to the group's development. Leaders should adapt their leadership styles to their followers. This was an innovative idea in leadership research. Hersey and Blanchard (1977), for example, created a model for situational leadership based on the premise that leaders should match work tasks with co-workers' competence. This theory of situational leadership assumes that participation and responsibility among co-workers can be gradually increased as their independence and competence increase. A later development of situational leadership is the Integrated Model of Group Development (Wheelan, 2005) as described in Chap. 6.

Transformational Leadership Theory

The idea of leadership as a process between leader and co-worker developed in the 1970s and the 1980s as theories about *transformational* leadership emerged (Bass, 1990). This new theory of leadership contrasted with the traditional idea of *transactional* leadership, in which an agreed-upon transaction existed between leaders and their co-workers. The leader might state the agreement as follows: "If you perform the work as we agreed, I will pay or reward you as agreed on the condition that I may check your work." In such a transaction, work control plays a larger role than work enthusiasm.

Transformational leadership research, in contrast, focused more on change and renewal than the earlier leadership research. This change in leadership focus required leaders to be proactive in involving co-workers in joint projects. Thus, leaders should have a positive attitude that supports, encourages, and inspires their co-workers. Transformational leadership is at present one of the most researched leadership theories and is further discussed in Chap. 7.

Shared Leadership Theories

A recent development of theory is to regard leadership as a collective phenomenon, in which leadership is based in people's interactions rather than in the actions of a single individual (Avolio et al., 2012; Raelin, 2016; Stacey & Mowles, 2016). In this research, all members of an organization are capable of exercising leadership, whether they have formal power or not. Research studies based on these distributed or shared leadership theories (e.g., Bolden, 2011; Denis et al., 2012; Gronn, 2002) are increasing. Paradoxically, in shared leadership, the manager's role and responsibilities become even more central in the leadership analysis. What is the formal leader's role if leadership is distributed among the many? Who should keep a cool head when tempers are flaring? How should such situations be handled and by whom? We return to these questions in later chapters.

All these leadership theories, existing in parallel, are relevant today. Leadership consultants refer to them, leadership researchers examine them (theoretically and empirically), university business students study them, and organizational managements use them in performance evaluations.

In summary, on the one hand, factors and conditions outside most leaders' control influence their leadership. On the other hand, leaders require certain traits and abilities that inspire co-workers' trust and acceptance of authority. Trust and authority are strongly related to the key dimension of leadership: the exercise of influence with sense and sensitivity.

How Is Leadership Exercised?

As a manager, how can you exert your influence in practice? Issues related to power are probably among the most intangible and emotionally challenging issues you will have to deal with in the managerial role. Planned and unplanned interactions between people with and without power can evoke strong emotions on both sides. As a manager, because of your position, you certainly have formal power (Yukl, 2013). Does this power also mean you have full control over situations or others? And what happens if you abuse your power?

Exercise of Power

As observed above, most definitions of leadership reference power in the context of influencing others and of being influenced by others. Influence is exercised in two ways. Either you establish group acceptance by your authority (see below) or you establish group acceptance by force. In the latter instance, as we all know, power is exercised against the will of others and with the threat of retaliation if resistance is offered. "If you do not do as I say, I will …." Many parents and children remember such uncomfortable, even painful, situations that often created even greater distance between them – between the powerful and the powerless.

Niccolò Machiavelli (1469–1527), the Italian statesman and political philosopher, wrote his most famous work, *The Prince*, in the early sixteenth century (Machiavelli, 2014). It is still studied today by decision-makers and business leaders who are interested in understanding power. In Machiavelli's conception, the ideal prince (i.e., leader) is a powerful and ruthless player who retains power so long as he has the consent of the governed (i.e., those without formal power). To achieve and maintain such power, an extreme form of political pragmatism is needed. The ends justify the means, according to Machiavelli. In a strong state, Machiavelli argues, the majority will benefit in the long-term from such authority. To achieve this end, betrayal, cruelty, and lies are not only allowed but also necessary.

The Prince still evokes strong emotions. Some of its advocates, who claim it reflects political and social reality, say Machiavelli was a pragmatic realist. They charge his critics with holding a naive and Utopian conception of how the world should be. Others argue that the work is merely a satire on the use of authoritarian power by leaders. Many interpretations are possible.

However, this authoritarian exercise of power can hardly be said to inspire creativity, trust, and commitment among a leader's followers. On the contrary, if leaders adopt a Machiavellian leadership style, they are more likely to provoke anger, resistance, and hatred in their co-workers. Co-workers may conceal these emotions to avoid negative consequences, but their clenched fists and whispered oaths reveal their real feelings. As leaders see their confidence capital decrease, they can easily fall into a downward spiral, in which they take still harsher disciplinary action. Empirical studies have found a connection between dictatorial managerial behavior and poorer co-worker mental and physical health and poorer organizational outcomes (Erickson et al., 2015; Nyberg, 2009).

Authority

Acting with authority is very different from exercising authoritarian power. When leaders act with authority, the power is legitimate. They have earned the trust required to act with authority. Yet it is pointless to say to someone: "From now on, look to me for authority." Authority, which derives from the trust of others, is premised on the assumption that those involved agree on the purpose of the requests/demands. In such situations, everyone may act with authority, regardless of position in the organization. Acting with authority means taking the initiative needed to achieve the overall purpose, and the agreed-upon goals of the organization. In Chap. 8, we describe this activity as being "in role." Leadership based on authority, as opposed to leadership based on the authoritarian exercise of power, contributes to the creation of trust and purpose in organizations and in society (Larsson et al., 2018; Reed & Bazalgette, 2006).

Organizational superiors give managers the authority to perform certain tasks requiring cooperation from their subordinates. Given this authority, managers may delegate tasks and responsibilities to others lower in the hierarchy. In certain authoritarian organizational cultures, managers may have no other option than formal delegation of tasks. Regardless of the circumstances, managers sometimes question their decision to delegate some tasks. Is the delegation in the best interests of the organization? How much responsibility has been delegated? What is the manager's role as far as the completion of the delegated tasks? Should the manager consult superiors? Do the co-workers sense a lack of conviction on the manager's part? These are questions managers should address before a major delegation of authority.

Striking an optimal balance between exercising power and acting with authority is not always easy. In some situations, managers should unhesitatingly use the authority assigned by their superiors (i.e., use their power to influence). Such is the case in crises when rapid responses are essential. In less critical situations, however, unilateral responses by managers (in which co-workers' contributions would have been helpful) can diminish co-workers' trust in their managers. A vicious circle is created, in which the more managers exercise authoritarian power, the more trust they lose. In such a situation, a time-out together with the co-workers is needed to re-establish authority and to rebuild trust.

References

Alvesson, M. (2017). *Reflexive leadership. Organising in an imperfect world.* Sage.

Alvesson, M., & Sveningsson, S. (2003). Managers doing leadership: The extra-ordinarization of the mundane. *Human Relations, 56*(12), 1435–1459. https://doi.org/10.1177/00187267035612001

Avolio, B. J., Sosik, J. J., & Berson, Y. (2012). Leadership models, methods and applications: Progress and remaining blind spots. In I. B. Weiner (red.), *Handbook of psychology*. Wiley.
Badaracco, J. L. (2002). *Leading quietly. An unorthodox guide to doing the right thing*. Harvard Business School Press.
Bass, B. M. (1990). From transactional to transformational leadership. Learning to share the vision. *Organizational Dynamics, 18*(3), 19–36.
Blake, R. R., & Mouton, J. S. (1985). *The managerial grid*. Gulf.
Bolden, R. (2011). Distributed leadership in organizations: A review of theory and research. *International Journal of Management Reviews, 13*(3), 251–269.
Costa, P. T., Jr., & McCrae, R. R. (1992). Four ways five factors are basic. *Personality and Individual Differences, 13*(6), 653–665.
Crevani, L., Lindgren, M., & Packendorff, J. (2010). Leadership, not leaders: On the study of leadership as practices and interactions. *Scandinavian Journal of Management, 26*, 77–86.
Denis, J.-L., Langley, A., & Sergi, V. (2012). Leadership in the plural. *The Academy of Management Annals, 6*(1), 211–283.
Dinh, J. E., Lord, R. G., Gardner, W. L., Meuser, J. D., Liden, R. C., & Hu, J. (2014). Leadership theory and research in the new millennium: Current theoretical trends and changing perspectives. *The Leadership Quarterly, 25*(1), 36–62.
Erickson, A., Shaw, B., Murray, J., & Branch, S. (2015). Destructive leadership: Causes, consequences and countermeasures. *Organizational Dynamics, 44*(4), 266–272.
George, J. M. (2000). Emotions and leadership. The role of emotional intelligence. *Human Relations, 53*, 1027–1055.
Grint, K. (1997). *Leadership. Classical, contemporary, and critical approaches*. Oxford University Press.
Gronn, P. (2002). Distributed leadership as a unit of analysis. *The Leadership Quarterly, 13*(4), 423–451.
Hersey, P., & Blanchard, K. H. (1977). *Management of organizational behaviors: Utilizing human resources*. Prentice-Hall.
Inceoglu, I., Thomas, G., Chu, C., Plans, D., & Gerbasi, A. (2018). Leadership behavior and employee well-being: An integrated review and a future research agenda. *The Leadership Quarterly, 29*(1), 179–202.
Jackson, B., & Parry, K. (2008). *A very short, fairly interesting and reasonably cheap book about studying leadership*. Sage.
Judge, T. A., Bono, J. E., Ilies, R., & Gerhardt, M. W. (2002). Personality and leadership: A qualitative and quantitative review. *Journal of Applied Psychology, 87*(4), 765–780.
Judge, T. A., Colbert, A. E., & Ilies, R. (2004). Intelligence and leadership: A quantitative review and test of theoretical propositions. *Journal of Applied Psychology, 89*(3), 542.
Koestenbaum, P. (2010). *Leadership. The inner side of greatness, a philosophy for leaders new and revised.* Wiley.
Larsson, G., Brandebo, M. F., & Nilsson, S. (2012). Destrudo-L: Development of a short scale designed to measure destructive leadership behaviours in a military context. *Leadership and Organization Development Journal, 33*(4), 383–400.
Larsson, G., Lundin, J., & Zander, A. (2018). *The leadership model – The art of matching individual and organizational characteristics*. Studentlitteratur.
Lewin, K., Lippit, R., & White, R. K. (1939). Patterns of aggressive behavior in experimentally created social climates. *Journal of Social Psychiatry, 10*, 271–301.
Maccoby, M. (1981). *The leader: A new face for American management*. Ballantine.
Machiavelli, N. (2014). *The prince*. Penguin Classics.
Meindl, J. (1995). The romance of leadership as a follower centric theory: A social constructionist approach. *The Leadership Quarterly, 6*(3), 329–341.
Meindl, J., Ehrlich, S. B., & Dukerich, J. M. (1985). The romance of leadership. *Administrative Science Quarterly, 30*(1), 78–102.
Northouse, P. G. (2007). *Leadership: Theory and practice* (4th ed.). Sage.

Nyberg, A. (2009). *The impact of managerial leadership on stress and health among employees.* Dissertation, Karolinska Institutet.

Raelin, J. (2016). *Leadership-as-practice. Theory and application.* Routledge.

Reed, B. D., & Bazalgette, J. L. (2006). Organisational role analysis at the Grubb Institute of Behavioural studies: Origins and development. In J. Newton, S. Long, & B. Sievers (Eds.), *Coaching in depth: The organisational role analysis approach.* Karnac.

Ronay, R., Oostrom, J. K., Lehmann-Willenbrock, N., Mayoral, S., & Rusch, H. (2019). Playing the trump card: Why we select overconfident leaders and why it matters. *The Leadership Quarterly, 30*(6), 101316.

Spector, B. A. (2016). Carlyle, Freud, and the great man theory more considered. *Leadership, 12*(2), 250–260.

Stacey, R. D., & Mowles, C. (2016). *Strategic management and organizational dynamics. The challenge of complexity to ways of thinking about organizations.* Pearson.

Wheelan, S. A. (2005). *Creating effective teams: A guide for members and leaders.* Sage.

Woods, S., & West, M. A. (2019). *The psychology of work and organisations* (3rd ed.). Cengage Publishing.

Yukl, G. (2013). *Leadership in organizations* (8th ed.). Pearson.

References

[illegible]

Emotions in the Workplace

4

Without attention to our emotions, we may act thoughtlessly.

In this chapter, we briefly review how emotions at work have been treated in the research literature. We also describe the power of emotions and address the importance of emotions when making reasoned and wise decisions. We emphasize that managers can improve their understanding and handling of emotions in the workplace.

Have you ever experienced anxiety or fear at work? Most people would probably admit that they have. Situations can vary in degree of anxiety from mild, in, for example, an appraisal conversation, to severe, for example, when you were scolded, justly or not, by your boss. How did such situations affect your capacity to think clearly? What happened to your experience of yourself? Even people in prestigious positions can report that they felt like an insecure pupil in front of their teacher.

Below is another example from a manager's perspective about the emotional consequences of gradually increased frustration:

> Imagine that a middle manager assigns a development project to a co-worker to manage. The manager is very confident about the co-worker's ability to handle this assignment. As project manager, the co-worker will lead the work, will interact with various actors with different areas of expertise, and will arrange and chair project meetings. The middle manager later hears that the project manager is having difficulty communicating with the group she manages and has even failed to attend an important meeting. It is rumored that the group members are confused and upset by this management style. The middle manager is greatly concerned about this situation with the project manager. Her own manager, who is eager for the results of the development project, is also annoyed. The middle manager's anxiety increases. She feels more and more tension in her neck and back. The middle manager wonders if she misjudged the project manager's competence. She worries that she misplaced her trust in the project manager. Are there other factors in play? Has another co-worker planted rumors to replace the project manager? As she ponders the whole situation, she imagines very disturbing scenarios. Her disappointment, anger, and worry increase. In an impromptu meeting, she abruptly and loudly reproaches the project manager in the presence of other co-workers. In a moment, a manageable situation has become a near out-of-control crisis.

C. Sandahl, M. von Knorring, *Managing with Sense and Sensitivity*,
https://doi.org/10.1007/978-3-031-24109-3_4

Sometimes our emotions triumph over our reason as in the example above. Afterward you may feel guilty when you have acted out your emotions abruptly. After a calm consideration of all the facts and the emotions involved, you will have a clearer picture of the incident. You may apologize for your mistake or try to correct it in some way. Should similar situations arise, you hope you can handle them more calmly and more reasonably.

Many such situations occur in work life – some less emotionally fraught, some more so. In each situation, as the manager, you need to be attuned to the emotions displayed. You have the power to protect your own and others' emotional well-being.

This chapter will be completely devoted to emotions. Managers are not psychotherapists or psychologists. Nor should one, as a manager, try to assume these roles. However, as a manager, you need to understand your own emotional reactions and your co-workers as well. Therefore, you will need some knowledge of emotions and how they affect you and others in the workplace. Why do emotions have such a strong influence in people's life, privately and at work? What is the significance of emotions for reason and the ability to make wise decisions?

Emotions and Work

It is perhaps naïve to ask which emotions arise at work. The context is irrelevant when identifying which work emotions are in focus; emotions are the same, regardless of where people interact. Despite this truism, leadership and organizational theories have long viewed the workplace as a kind of emotionless zone. Research on leadership and organizations has been described as "passion-free" (Gabriel, 1999) and "emotionally anorexic" (Fineman, 1997). Sigmund Freud (1921) concluded there was "too much organization in organizations" for them to be worthy of any greater interest.

The bureaucratic ideal, which dominated much of the twentieth century, may in large part explain this lack of interest in emotions in the workplace. In the early twentieth century, the German sociologist and economist Max Weber (1864–1920) concluded that bureaucracy, with its carefully designed functions, was the most efficient, effective, and superior form of organization, not least in its exercise of public power. However, Weber warned that the consequences of bureaucracy in its most goal-rationalizing and instrumentally driven form could be destructive to mankind (Weber, 1948).

While organizational bureaucracy in some form is indispensable – certainly in public life – it is increasingly problematic to describe organizations as "passion-free." The view of organizations as "emotional arenas" (Gabriel, 1999), where emotions, fantasies, ambitions, conflicts, guilt, and joy are constantly present (Firth-Cozens & Mowbray, 2001), has considerable support. An awareness of the importance of emotions vis à vis the leadership role has increased in recent years. *Leadership Quarterly*, one of the most respected leadership journals, devoted issues to emotions and leadership in 2002 and 2015. The articles in these issues described current research on emotions and leadership as a rich research area with a variety of theoretical perspectives as well as a range of methods (Connelly & Gooty, 2015; Humphrey, 2002).

As noted in Chap. 2, research on the importance of emotions in leadership has increased noticeably in the twenty-first century. Five scientific literature reviews on leadership and emotions were, for example, published in the years 2010–2018: Ashkanasy & Humphrey, 2011; Berkovich & Eyal, 2015; Gooty et al., 2010; Rajah et al., 2011; and Tse et al., 2018. This research address not only the managers' emotions but also the effect of managers' control and display of emotion on co-workers' emotion regulation and work performance.

Mainly two questions are posed in these reviews. How well do managers understand their own emotions? And How well do managers express these emotions appropriately in given situations? Researchers agree that these questions must be answered for creating harmonious relationships between managers and co-workers.

To some extent, however, the leadership and emotions research is complicated by its narrow focus on satisfying relationships (Lindebaum & Jordan, 2014). One criticism of such research is that researchers seem content to look only for positive relationship evidence, for example, relationships in which managers inspire co-workers, and vice versa. Their assumption is that positive feelings produce positive outcomes and negative feelings produce negative outcomes. This assumption is obviously not true. For example, how can one be authentically positive when things go wrong? The journal *Human Relations* devoted one of its 2014 issues to the so-called workplace emotional asymmetries framed around the question of when it is good to feel bad and when it is bad to feel good (Lindebaum & Jordan, 2014).

Anger, for example, in and of itself is neither good nor bad. Anger is situation dependent. If managers or co-workers perceive injustices or discover unethical actions at work, anger is an understandable response – even if their angry response disturbs their mental equilibrium. A repressed, even passive, response may not be healthy or advisable. The same observation applies to other emotions, for example, discontent, envy, and guilt. The controlled and nonconfrontational expression of such emotions can even strengthen social ties in the workplace. These emotions may be perceived as negative but can actually help us understand how an individual – a manager or a co-worker – perceives a specific situation.

The business world has also noted the importance of emotions in the workplace. Even a cursory Internet search reveals numerous websites for business schools/universities, consultancy firms, and popular management journals that promote training and education in what are variously described as interpersonal skills, people skills, and social skills. A typical example of such language is the following from the Swedish trade journal for managers, *Chef* (October 2021): "Contrary to the traditional view of leadership, many organizations now want leaders who show compassion and vulnerability – someone who dares to experiment by trying different, forward-looking solutions. We must get used to a future with constantly changing challenges where we are comfortable in leading in times of uncertainty" [in translation].

Another example comes from the Swedish financial newspaper, *Dagens industri*, which published an article calling on managers to let their emotions flow. According to a review (Mellqvist, 2008), the article proclaimed it was time for "modern managers to drop their poker faces" [in translation]. However, managers who drop their poker faces take a risk. The public response to people who express their emotions openly can be harsh. They may be shamed and humiliated, because expressions of public remorse and grief may be interpreted as signs of weakness. It often takes considerable courage to express one's emotions in public – even when such expressions are needed as well as justified.

The Romans had a word for "head" (in the literal sense): *caput*, which is etymologically related to the word "chef," which is the Swedish word for manager, or the head of the restaurant kitchen in English. Another English derivation of this Latin word is "captain" as used, for example, in the term "captains of industry." However, English also uses the word "head" to refer to heads of organizations. It seems that there is a common understanding that managers need to use their heads, i.e., to be able to think. At times, it is necessary to keep emotions at bay when decisions are made. Expressions such as "It hit her in the head" and "Anger went to his head" illustrate less than optimal outcomes when emotions "take over" reason.

To let the emotions rule completely is of course very problematic. However, the other extreme, not to take your emotions into account is not a solution. Many managers regrettably make the mistake of completely distancing themselves from their emotions when they make decisions. They then cause problems for themselves, for their co-workers, and for their organizations, because they do not take the whole situation into consideration.

To understand the power of emotional dynamics in the workplace, managers need to learn why emotions can have such power over their lives. Therefore, we explore in depth the world of emotions in the next sections.

Our Affects, Emotions, and Feelings

It is challenging to differentiate among affects, emotions, and feelings. Even researchers struggle with defining them separately (Levy Berg, 2009). It is often said that feelings are the mental experience of an affect and emotions are the cognitive evaluation of the affect, including previous experiences with it. Donald Nathanson, an internationally renowned emotion researcher, defined affect in terms of biology, feeling in terms of psychology, and emotion in terms of biography (Nathanson, 1992). For further simplification, in this book we refer to "feelings" in the broadest sense to include various aspects that have to do with how aware you are of an affect, how well you tolerate it, and how you express it emotionally and verbally.

The primary affects are inherent in human biological nature. However, people are much more than nature and biology. The human condition includes the social, psychological, and spiritual/existential elements of life. In creating cultures that support long-term survival, humankind has tried to master biologically controlled human impulses and forces in various ways. Emotions are therefore far more complex than the primary affects that exist as pure physical responses, no matter how much we try to ignore or deny them.

In everyday language, when we refer to our feelings, we are usually describing something more than pure affects. Once an affect is present – often early in life – you become aware of how that affect feels and how others perceive it in you. These memories are stored so that the next time the affect occurs, you connect your previous experience with the affect. Thus, each affect is colored by events from your life. In some childhood environments, for example, it may be forbidden to react with anger or sadness, while the same emotions are accepted in other contexts. People's spontaneous expressions of enjoyment and interest may be welcomed or punished, depending on the environment.

Families deal with emotions variously. Emotions are also treated variously in different cultures, religions, and political circumstances. These differences are generally reflected in the specific social norms of countries and cultures. National and social histories, as well as people's personal histories, play a major role in determining how people connect with and express their emotions. The recognition and expression of emotions help shape our personalities (which, of course, are also genetically determined in a certain sense), even though the biological affects are the same in all people.

Early in life, humans develop typical coping behaviors (i.e., patterns) in response to such emotions. These behaviors are our best responses to challenging situations when these emotions are aroused. Because we develop these behaviors in different family constellations and contexts, they become deeply personal and idiosyncratic. According to the American psychiatrist and researcher of child development Daniel Stern (1995), such coping behaviors can be described as "ways of being with the other." Stern argues that a few typical coping behaviors characterize and express our personalities. Solms (2021) claims that these coping behaviors become automatic as part of our procedural, long-term memory. As unconscious memories, they are repeated endlessly. If the "ways of being with the other" that we develop over the years do not create problems, we have no reason to change them. Unfortunately, when these "ways of being with the other" create problems in adult life, we do not understand why simply because the reasons behind the coping behaviors are unconscious. As a manager, it is easy to repeat negative behaviors in response to certain affectively loaded situations, unless one is confronted with the adverse consequences and offered an opportunity for reflection and behaviour change.

The Biological Basis of Emotions

The British evolutionary researcher Charles Darwin (1809–1882) drew attention to the importance of emotions in his study of survival among high-ranking monkeys and herd animals. He concluded that species survival depends, in part, on fear of that which threatens life and health, on the avoidance of poisonous plants, and on the exploration of new locations favorable to habitation. In contemporary times, people have associated Darwin's ideas on the survival of the species with the biological origin and function of emotions.

Building on Darwin, the American psychologist Silvan Tomkins (1911–1991), the Estonian/North American neuroscientist Jaak Panksepp (1943–2017), and others have contributed to a deeper understanding of emotions, their biological origin, their survival, and evolutionary value. Panksepp, for example, discovered that humans share our basic instincts and the accompanying affects with all mammals (Solms, 2021). Affects, as defined by Tomkins, are the physiological responses to stimuli in the environment. The responses include fear, rage, joy, sadness, shame, and a few more. The same muscles in the face are activated for each of these primary affects in all human beings. Researchers agree that culture and upbringing can modify the intensity of the affects, although there is disagreement on how many affects exist – seven, nine, or some other number. The main point is that affects, because of their universal characteristics, are relatively easy to read.

However, people require face-to-face encounters to read other people's affects. We need to make eye contact and to observe other people's body language if we are to inspire trust and create connections. When we enter rooms, very quickly we observe others; we can tell who is sad, angry, unengaged, hostile, etc. In the digital age of online meetings, such visual observations are considerably more difficult to do.

The Power of Emotions: The Primary Affects

Stemming from the research on affects, researchers have further investigated the primary affects related to the power of emotions (Ekman & Friesen, 2015; Nathanson, 1992). As mentioned, an affect is the immediate physiological response that follows a sensory stimulus. The response reaches the central part of the brain faster than the awareness of the sensory stimulus. When we experience the affect, we define it as a feeling. We thus become aware of our responses only after the incident that caused the response. These reflex responses in certain situations (e.g., our response to fear of the unknown) have functioned as survival mechanisms for humans for millennia.

In this section, we describe seven primary affects based on our integration of several research tracks (e.g., research by Ekman, Panksepp, and Tomkins). The primary affects are expressed by their specific bodily and physiological reactions. It is possible, for example, to link each affect with a specific body posture or with a characteristic facial muscle movement (Ekman, 1992). When comparing different cultures, researchers have found people are quite similar in their body and facial expression of affects. Affects, such as rage, fear, and joy, activate the same facial muscles among all humans independent of where in the world they live or where they are born. However, cultural or family influences may modify the intensity of the expression. In some cultures, for example, the open expression of anger is undesired. In such cultures, people learn early in life to inhibit the expressions of irritation, resentment, rage, and similar emotions. Then, it can be almost impossible for an outsider to discover the activation of the face muscles associated to anger, but they will be easily identified with, for example, electromyography (EMG).

The way people handle emotionally charged situations, on the other hand, varies, depending, among other things, on their ability to recognize emotions (i.e., how aware people are of the affect they present in different situations). Am I sad or angry? This is not always a simple question to answer. Probably you have experienced the somewhat confusing situation, when you have tried to comfort a weeping co-worker or spouse and abruptly were sent away and asked to mind your own business. People also have different levels of emotional tolerance. They may not need to act on all the emotions they experience. Nevertheless, the ability to express emotions in words is important for dealing with emotionally charged situations.

Because all primary affects have survival value, you cannot categorize them as either positive or negative. Perhaps a better way to categorize them is by their primary function. Translated to the workplace, one can think in terms of their cohesive or distancing effects. Therefore, we present the seven affects in three categories: cohesive, distancing, and neutral affects.

Four Cohesive Affects

Interest

The affect interest is associated with Panksepp's seeking instinct, which serves survival among mammals (i.e., seeking food or a mate). This affect, which suggests a curiosity that can increase to excitement and enthusiasm, triggers joyful activities of exploring, thinking, and learning. In essence, the affect interest is the bridge between sense and sensitivity, in that it is a prerequisite for thoughtful consideration, analysis, and creativity when not acted on impulsively. As a manager, you might experience this when you are completely absorbed by an unexpected opportunity. The trick is to be able to keep a sane distance and at the same time to transfer the feeling of enthusiasm to your fellow co-workers. The affect interest is the corner stone for work motivation.

Enjoyment-Joy

The affect enjoyment-joy causes people to approach something or respond to someone. Think of a baby's smile that spontaneously prompts the caregiver to smile in return. This affect creates a pleasant and rewarding feeling that reinforces social behaviors and trust. It is related to Panksepp's care instinct, which triggers tenderness and love, and to the play instinct, which serves cooperation and teamwork. The survival value of enjoyment-joy is obvious in its ability to reinforce attachment behaviors for the protection of offspring. At work, a smile contributes to cohesion and mutual support. While other affects become more intense as the experience intensifies, enjoyment-joy, by contrast, decreases in intensity and leads to serenity; at its maximum, the affect is therefore thought to link to human spirituality. With respect to the survival of the species theory, enjoyment-joy strengthens the bonds between people, not least between children and parents but certainly also at the workplace. If you ever have experienced a well-functioning work group, you will know how important enjoyment-joy is for productivity and work satisfaction. This will be further explored in Chap. 6. The intensification of enjoyment-joy also has an existential dimension, because the affect relates to the very essence of life and the experience of context and meaning. Context and meaning are too often overlooked, even in the workplace. We return to these two concepts in Chap. 8.

Sadness

The affect sadness, the feeling of loneliness, anxiety, and sorrow, relates to Panksepp's panic instinct, which is the reaction to the severance of attachment bonds. You hear sadness in nature, for example, in the frantic baby bird's chirp when it falls from the nest – a cry for help. The human baby's cry at birth indicates the distress and anguish of the newborn's response to intense stimulation. The anxiety related to the fear or threat of abandonment differs from the anxiety triggered by the affect fear (see below). Among adults, sadness also binds people when friends and relatives witness a sad person's crumpled position, easily recognizable sad expression, and lack of energy. The instinct tells us to give care, to comfort (McClusky, 2005). At work, sadness can be experienced in many kinds of situations, for example, when somebody has failed to accomplish a task, when one feels excluded, or when work has lost its meaning. As a manager, it is important to be responsive to expressions of sadness, to reinforce conversations, and to listen and take the time to allow the feelings to fade away. Confronted in such an empathic way, the affect will serve cohesion at the workplace. If ignored, the opposite will happen. The person will feel rejected and abandoned, which in turn will feed mistrust and undermine motivation for work.

Sadness varies in intensity from mild depression to severe depression. When people are sad because of another's death, the bonds between them may strengthen as they seek comfort together. However, it can be expected that sadness may turn to despair in such reunions. Yet despair is not necessarily something to fear; despair can be a normal part of grieving that is facilitated by the presence of others. When we observe people's dependency on others' acknowledgment of their despair, we understand how mental well-being is threatened by such tragic losses. Many primary affects are observable, even in herd animals, but sadness is especially easy to recognize. Man, however, is the only animal that weeps (Vingerhoets, 2013).

Shame

The physical expressions of the affect shame are easily recognizable: people tend to look down, avoid eye contact, and often blush. People who are ashamed sometimes say: "I wanted to sink through the floor." People may feel shame, for example, when they have said or done something humiliating, when others ignore them, or when others reject them. This affect is related to Panksepp's play instinct, when a joyous interaction abruptly ends in frustration, anger, or sadness, which often is the case with children. Shame, which is experienced when joy or excitement is thwarted, focuses attention on causes. Most people have experienced shame at work. Think, for example, of a situation when a first-line or middle manager has been invited to the top management team to present a project idea, and few listens, and those who listen dismiss it all as an impossible idea. The shame can obviously trigger other affects such as rage or sadness also in adults.

Shame also relates to the survival of the species theory. The group creates acceptable and unacceptable standards of behavior – what is allowed and what is taboo (i.e., shameful). At work it is not always easy to know what the norms are. By painful experiences of shame, one gradually learns. Individuals, whose self-preservation is linked to the group's survival, feel shame if they violate accepted behavior standards. Shame has yet another function: it protects self-identity by revealing who one is. Shaming experiences strengthen people's inner dialogues about their behavior and increase their awareness of the boundaries of the self (Harwood et al., 2012). How embarrassing and awkward, shame can still be a learning experience.

Even in destructive family groups, in quarrelsome work groups, or in certain sects, shame can be the glue that binds the members together. Members who speak negatively about other members may be shunned or silenced. Such criticism is therefore usually avoided (see the groupthink discussion in Chap. 6). In this way, the threat of shame binds the group together.

Two Distancing Affects

In the same way as some affects have the function of reinforcing cohesion, some affects have the power to create distances between people. Yet, from a biological perspective, distance-creating affects – such as fear and anger – support the survival of the species.

Fear

The affect fear can range from vague anxiety (whose causes are difficult to pinpoint) to paralyzing terror (whose causes are often clearly identifiable). When an individual experiences extreme fear, the sympathetic nervous system in the body is mobilized. The heart pumps faster, the pupils dilate, and physical energy is directed to the most vital functions – the functions needed for fighting, fleeing, or freezing. Fear is necessary for survival. A lack of fear when faced with danger can be life-threatening for oneself and for others. It is important to be vigilant to all kinds of threats in the work environment, including threats to the business itself. No actions would be taken to counteract such threats without at least some moderate degree of fear. If one as a manager is influenced too much by fear, one needs urgent assistance and help to contain the feelings. If a manager is unable to contain feelings of fear, it will easily spread to co-workers, and in the end very few in the organization will be able to think clearly. As will be explained later in this chapter, emotions are contagious. Machiavellian type of leaders with an autocratic style uses fear to exercise power. High-ranking officers can easily become like young pupils in front of authoritarian political leaders.

Anger

The affect anger can range from extreme irritation to all-consuming rage. Anger provokes powerful physical responses. When we experience this affect, we may coldly distance ourselves from others, we may loudly taunt and criticize others, or we may aggressively attack others. The physiological expressions of anger include red faces, raised blood pressure, clenched jaws, muscle tension, and faster respiration. The throat may dilate as if our primal instinct is preparing us to frighten a predator with our screams – a response that has certainly served evolutionary survival. In the "jungle" of the contemporary workplace, however, we need to find other ways to manage the rage provoked by our anger.

If your body responds to anger with these physical responses, you may think you are on the verge of a violent outburst. You may want to strike someone or kick something. It is not unusual to have these thoughts when one's freedom of action is threatened, especially when one is thwarted from trying to achieve a certain goal. However, it is important to distinguish anger from destructive aggressive behavior that often results in physical assault or property damage. Anger increases the risk of this type of aggression. Even mild irritation should be managed because, if linked to powerlessness, frustration, and failure, it can easily turn to less manageable expressions of anger.

Anger in the range of irritation is common at workplaces. It is the natural response to frustration, and it should not be repressed. As a manager, you need to know what caused the frustration, and if you as a manager is the frustrated part, you need to understand what it was all about. Anger used as information and contained to an endurable degree is the manager's best friend!

A Neutral Affect

Surprise

Surprise is a neutral affect, because it can cause both cohesive and distancing responses. When surprised by events, ideas, or other people, most of us pause to reflect on the situation. After consideration, we may either draw away or approach nearer (physically or metaphorically). In other words, surprise is an affect that can relate to the affects of fear and interest. Depending, among other things, on their previous experiences, people may react very differently to the same surprising situation. One individual may respond defensively and fearfully; another may respond with curiosity and interest. As a manager, you should never lose your capacity for surprise. It is the key to many opportunities.

The Body: Emotions and Experiences

As we have emphasized above, the primary affects are characterized by the fact that they reveal themselves in our physical responses. These physical responses also reveal who we are – our sense of ourselves (Stern, 1985). In developmental psychology, for example, concepts such as the "body" and the "skin ego" (Aron & Anderson, 1998) are important for describing how the body reflects our experience with the external world. We retain physical experiences from birth and even from the womb. How we as adults react to the external world to some extent depends on how we were held as infants. For a child, as well as for an adult, the skin is a clear boundary with the external world. Our skin is also a sensitive "mind" that responds to how we are touched.

The combination of affects and bodily sensations forms memories that shape our view of the world. This process continues in our interactions with people throughout our lives as new emotional experiences confirm or alter our previous emotional experiences. All forms of psychotherapy, for example, are premised on the idea that by learning to handle certain situations differently, one can learn about (and alter) basic patterns that create relationship problems or issues. We need not be at the mercy of our feelings; we can learn to make choices independent of them. The originator of systems-centered therapy, Yvonne Agazarian (1929–2017) argued that sometimes we need to pause and think about the path we are on and the path we should take: the path of exploration or the path of defense (Agazarian et al., 2021). Do we want to be more open, or do we want to close down? Often, simply being aware of what path we want to choose begins the process of change.

A colleague who treats patients once commented: "If for some reason we stop listening to our body signals, our bodies will eventually cry out even louder." Sometimes our psychological defenses are so powerful that everyone, except the person in question, can see the problem. People's inability to identify, experience, and name their emotions eventually puts them at risk of psychosomatic symptoms, such as headaches, heart/vascular problems, and stomach, back, and neck pain. They may also experience an increase in troublesome mental symptoms such as restlessness and anxiety. Ultimately, some people try risky solutions to alleviate such physical and mental symptoms, including excessive alcohol consumption or excessive physical activity (Bullington, 2013). The North American psychologist Victor Schermer argues that the way we understand others is based on embodied perceptions. The human body attunes to the feelings of others. In his view, intuition and gut feelings provide a lot of reliable information (Schermer, 2018).

Emotional Intelligence: What Is It?

If managers and co-workers are to act thoughtfully, they need to reflect on their emotions and what these emotions mean for themselves and others. How do we know if we experience a particular affect? This is not always easy. What happens in our bodies when we are angry, sad, or joyful? What does an emotion mean in terms of one's previous experiences? Do we really react to something in the here and now, or are we reacting to "old" emotions from the past? Can the same emotion have a different meaning for someone else? How should emotions be expressed? Which words best describe certain emotions? How can emotions be shared with others?

A person's ability to answer such questions is sometimes described as emotional intelligence (EQ). EQ is a collective term for several different abilities that are important for how we relate to emotions – our own emotions and others' emotions. Leadership researchers have studied EQ intensively, and numerous books and articles in various fields, both scientific and popular, focus on EQ (George, 2000; Ginsberg & Davies, 2007; Rajah et al., 2011; Serrat, 2017).

Most descriptions of EQ include three basic elements: (1) the ability to identify emotions in oneself and others, (2) the ability to relate to one's own and others' emotions, and (3) the ability to manage emotions and their expression (George, 2000; Goleman, 1995; Rajah et al., 2011; Salovey & Mayer, 1990). Below, we focus on the first of the three elements: the ability to identify emotions in oneself and others.

The Ability to Identify Emotions in Oneself and Others

The ability to identify emotions in oneself and others is the basis for understanding emotions and responding adequately to them. It may seem obvious that you know, for example, when you are angry, desperate, or ashamed. However, such self-awareness is not always easy. In psychology, the term alexithymia is sometimes used for the inability to identify and describe one's own emotions. A total inability to identify emotions is relatively uncommon. However, while most people can identify their own emotions, it is not certain that they always do. Perhaps you, like others, in the heat of an argument have insisted aggressively: "I am not angry!" You are completely convinced the other party is the angry person. Later, when you calm down, you take control of your emotions. You admit, at least to yourself, that you were angry. The problem was not your inability to identify an emotion. The problem was that you used denial, a common psychological defense. And you even accused the other party of the very emotion you were experiencing, which is projection, another common defense. But you were indeed very angry.

Projection is a defense mechanism people use to deny their own emotions and to attribute them to others. Using projection, one defends oneself from some emotion by pointing to that emotion in someone else. Very often these are negative emotions, such as anger, contempt, disgust, or shame. The ability, and willingness, to admit to your emotions, instead of projecting them on others, means that you take responsibility for them.

In hiring managers, it is not entirely uncommon to observe an imbalance between the intellectual and the emotional intelligence of the applicants. The following case of a job applicant we call Michael is an example:

> Michael was an applicant for a position as a senior manager at a medium-sized technology company. According to his resume, he was skilled and experienced in several relevant areas. He performed well in his interviews and prehire assessment tests. However, his work references revealed he had some personnel difficulties with his co-workers, because he seemed not to be in touch with his own emotions. Nevertheless, after the employment consultant and the employer reviewed Michael's application, interviews, and tests, he was hired. They

concluded that his excellent work skills, his intelligence, and his analytical abilities in combination with his considerable work experience outweighed his shortcomings as a manager of co-workers. The company simply needed him and did not want a competitor to hire him. However, at the same time, the company made another critical decision. A currently employed co-worker was added to Michaels's team. This individual, who had the people skills that Michael lacked, would act as the intermediary between Michael and the team members. In essence, the company's solution was shared leadership.

Michael lacked the ability to identify and respond to co-workers' emotions. His previous work references indicated that his insufficient empathic capacity had created interpersonal difficulties with the people whose work he managed. He had, however, abilities that, to some extent, compensated for this shortcoming. In the conversation with the employment consultant, Michael understood he did not (at least not yet …) have sufficient empathy to perform all the required managerial tasks satisfactorily. This conversation, while perhaps painful for Michael, was necessary so that he could learn from his previous experiences and develop in his new position through the experience of shared leadership.

Emotions Are Contagious

Face-to-face interactions with others provoke various responses from us. Sometimes, in meetings with others, it seems as if they have a depressing effect on us. Others' dark moods seem to suffocate us, as if a heavy, wet blanket smothered everything we do and think. Contrast that response when others' good spirits are so contagious that we are happy just being around them.

Of course, the power we give others over our lives is quite complex in its origins. Research shows that there is a neurobiological basis behind what is sometimes called emotional contagion (Hatfield et al., 1994). Emotional contagion refers to a congenital, unconscious tendency to imitate others and to experience another's being. Most people probably recognize this tendency in themselves. Perhaps you began a conversation with someone you did not know well. At first, you acted naturally by just being yourself. Suddenly you found yourself assuming the same physical posture as the other person. Both of you were sitting face-to-face, chin in hands, furrowing brows – and feeling a bit ridiculous.

However, as this example illustrates, emotional contagion doesn't just involve imitation of experiences. Recent research on emotions has turned some familiar notions about emotional contagion upside down. One may think that experiences provoke emotions, but research has shown that emotions are also provoked by imitating physical expressions. When another person smiles, for example, we smile in response. We also feel happy. Studies show that emotional contagion occurs not only on the individual level but also on the group level. Recent research has also shown that emotional states spread in the workplace (Anger Elfenbein, 2014; Bull Schaefer & Palanski, 2014; Johnson, 2008, 2009; Visser et al., 2013).

Emotions are contagious in different ways. Negative emotions, for example, seem more contagious and provoke stronger response behaviors than positive emotions. People also vary in their contagious effects. For example, people in leadership positions seem to be more powerful emotion spreaders than those in subordinate positions (Sy et al., 2005). Positive emotions spread if co-workers can identify with honest and reliable leaders. Negative emotions spread if co-workers identify with dishonest and unreliable leaders (Avolio & Gardner, 2005).

Like other infections, emotional contagion can be harmful to our well-being. For example, some individuals are extremely sensitive to the emotional needs of others and less sensitive to their own needs. The Swiss psychoanalyst Alice Miller (1923–2010) wrote an important book on this topic: *The Drama of the Gifted Child* (1996). In this book, Miller explores how children's deafness to their own feelings works as a survival mechanism against self-absorbed and insensitive parents. Given the potential damage from emotional contagion with such a background, one might need help to set limits on other people's emotional signals and, in a certain sense, become insensitive to their needs. At minimum, one should establish a certain distance from these negative emotional signals to attend to one's own needs and emotions.

Emotions Are Information

Because how we are biologically constructed, we immediately recognize and, to some extent, experience others' emotions. Therefore, it is possible, and sometimes necessary, to pause and reflect on such emotions. We may ask ourselves questions such as the following:

1. What does this emotion reveal about me?
2. What does this emotion reveal about others?
3. What does this emotion reveal about the situation in general?
4. What does this emotion reveal about the work group?
5. What does this emotion reveal about the organization?

Thus, our emotions act as signaling systems. Your emotions send important information to you, as a manager, which can help you to analyze and interpret what is going on around you. You have an opportunity to capture and attend to the emotional processes and dynamics in the organization you lead. Your responses can be crucial for the people you lead and for the performance of your organization.

Emotions Are the Prerequisite for Sound Judgment

For many years, emotions and reason were widely regarded as unrelated when considering human responses and decisions. Yet some philosophers have commented on the importance of emotions in relation to reason, rationality, and morality. David Hume (1711–1776), the Scottish economist and historian, was notably one of these philosophers. More recent research shows that emotions, in addition to their propensity to pose threats to sound judgment, can also be the prerequisites for sound judgment.

The Portuguese American neurologist Antonio Damasio described this phenomenon in his book *Descartes' Error: Emotion, Reason, and the Human Brain* (1994). In the book, Damasio shows, in a series of examples from his own and others' research, how reason and judgment relate to people's emotional capacity and how a certain type of limited brain damage can influence emotional life and decision-making. Damasio recounts the following patient trauma.

> Elliot was a 30-year-old man who had a top position at a company. He performed competently and responsibly. He was also happily married and enjoyed family life. However, Elliot's mental behavior suddenly began to change. He was then diagnosed with a tumor in the frontal brain lobe. Elliot could no longer make reasoned decisions. In addition, he began to act unethically, immorally, and irresponsibly – at work and at home. Eventually, he lost his job and his family. After the tumor was removed surgically, he once again performed excellently on tests of logical intelligence, and he even scored above average. Elliot could use his reason to solve ethical problems and could anticipate the social consequences of his actions. Nevertheless, he could not make decisions requiring sound judgment.

The medical explanation was that Elliot still lacked some capacity. He was strangely unaffected by what had happened to him because he had lost an emotional capacity. Damasio concluded that Elliot had lost the intimate interplay between emotion and reason that is required to make decisions and to function as a social being.

Damasio's example is, of course, very dramatic and possibly unique. However, it is still true that we cannot (and do not) make some decisions based only on cognitively rational arguments. It is interesting how often, nevertheless, we explain our decisions as if they were based solely on intellectual analysis. It is a very human tendency, but it is an illusory one. The Israeli psychologist and Nobel laureate Daniel Kahneman has contributed to our understanding of the relation between quick, intuitive, and emotional decisions and slower and deliberate decisions in his book, *Thinking, Fast and Slow* (2011). His argument is that quick thought processes can be the most efficient ones if the prerequisites are the same and the context unchanged. However, if they are not, we need to reflect and think through the situation in all its complexity before we carefully decide how to proceed. Emotions, such as an uncomfortable gut feeling, can be red flags. Now is time for reflection and thinking.

Emotional Work

We do not, of course, support making decisions based only on emotions. Obviously, there is an emotional and / or value-based component in most decision-making scenarios. The challenge is to examine the complexity of such scenarios and do what can be described as emotional work. This work requires a tolerance for the inevitable frustration and anxiety that arise – the "negative capacity" as it is called (Simpson & French, 2006). Negative capacity, which is closely linked to the concept of emotional work, is about self-awareness and self-development, both of which assume decision-makers take the time needed to reflect on their emotional responses (Nesbit, 2012).

Emotional work differs somewhat from empathy, which concerns the identification of emotions. Emotional work also involves assessments of how others may react. Sometimes one may need to tone down one's own reactions or, in some other cases, express more emotion than is really felt (Iszatt-White, 2009). Given a superficial understanding of oneself and others, such processes can degenerate into manipulation and the negative exercise of power. Emotional work, therefore, also includes ethical reflection aimed at drawing attention to the values that are at stake, such as integrity and human dignity.

Emotions also provide us with information about what is right or wrong. The American philosopher Martha Nussbaum has developed a theory of emotions as value judgments. She maintains we must pay close attention to the facts of a situation if we are not to be misled by our emotions. Situations should be evaluated by taking a reflective (metaphorical) walk back and forth between reason and emotions (Nussbaum, 2001).

Many of us today, who observe certain world events with shock and horror, may claim, with no small justification, that if we fail to use some aspect of our emotions in decision-making, we risk making hasty, even knee-jerk responses. Emotional work can give us grounds to pause and rethink while we decide on a reasoned course of action.

References

Agazarian, Y. M., Gantt, S. P., & Carter, F. B. (2021). *Systems-centered training*. Routledge.

Anger Elfenbein, H. (2014). The many faces of emotional contagion: An affective process theory of affective linkage. *Organizational Psychology Review, 4*(4), 326–362.

Aron, L., & Anderson, F. S. (1998). *Relational perspectives on the body*. The Analytic Press.

Ashkanasy, N. M., & Humphrey, R. H. (2011). Current emotion research in organizational behavior. *Emotion Review, 3*(2), 214–224.

Avolio, B. J., & Gardner, W. L. (2005). Authentic leadership development: Getting to the root of positive forms of leadership. *Leadership Quarterly, 16*, 315–338.

Berkovich, I., & Eyal, O. (2015). Educational leaders and emotions: An international review of empirical evidence. *Review of Educational Research, 85*(1), 129–167.

Bull Schaefer, R. A., & Palanski, M. E. (2014). Emotional contagion at work: An in-class experiential activity. *Journal of Management Education, 38*(4), 533–559.

Bullington, J. (2013). *The expression of the psychosomatic body from a phenomenological perspective*. Springer.

Connelly, S., & Gooty, J. (2015). Leading with emotion: An overview of the special issue on leadership and emotions. *The Leadership Quarterly, 26*(4), 485–488.

Damasio, A. (1994). *Descartes' Error. Emotion, reason and the human brain*. Penguin.

Ekman, P. (1992). An argument for basic emotions. *Cognition & Emotion, 6*, 169–200.

Ekman, P., & Friesen, W. V. (2015). *Unmasking the face. A guide to recognizing emotions from facial expressions*. Malor Books.

Fineman, S. (Ed.). (1997). *Emotion in organizations*. Sage.

Firth-Cozens, J., & Mowbray, D. (2001). Leadership and the quality of care. *Quality in Health Care, 10*(Suppl. II), 3–117.
Freud, S. (1921). Group psychoanalysis and the analysis of the ego. In S. Freud (Ed.), *Civilization, society and religion*. Penguin.
Gabriel, Y. (1999). *Organizations in depth. The psychoanalysis of organizations*. Sage.
George, J. M. (2000). Emotions and leadership. The role of emotional intelligence. *Human Relations, 53*, 1027–1055.
Ginsberg, R., & Davies, T. G. (2007). *The human side of leadership. Navigating emotions at work*. Praeger.
Goleman, D. (1995). *Emotional intelligence*. Bantam Books. ISBN 978-0-553-38371-3
Gooty, J., Connelly, S., Griffith, J., & Gupta, A. (2010). Leadership, affect and emotions: A state of the science review. *The Leadership Quarterly, 21*(6), 979–1004.
Harwood, I., Stone, W., & Pines, M. (2012). *Self-experiences in group, revisited. Affective attachments, intersubjective regulations, and human understanding*. Routledge.
Hatfield, E., Cacioppo, J. T., & Rapson, R. L. (1994). *Emotional contagion*. Cambridge University Press.
Humphrey, R. D. (2002). The many faces of emotional leadership. *The Leadership Quarterly, 13*(5), 493–504.
Iszatt-White, M. (2009). Leadership as emotional labour: The effortful accomplishment of valuing practices. *Leadership, 5*(4), 447–467.
Johnson, S. K. (2008). I second that emotion: Effects of emotional contagion and affect at work on leader and follower outcomes. *The Leadership Quarterly, 19*, 1–19.
Johnson, S. K. (2009). Do you feel what I feel? Mood contagion and leadership outcomes. *The Leadership Quarterly, 20*, 814–827.
Kahneman, D. (2011). *Thinking, fast and slow*. Farrar, Straus and Giroux.
Levy Berg, A. (2009). *Affect-focused body psychotherapy for patients with generalised anxiety disorder.* Dissertation. Karolinska Institutet.
Lindebaum, D., & Jordan, P. J. (2014). When it can be good to feel bad and bad to feel good: Exploring asymmetries in workplace emotional outcomes. *Human Relations, 67*(9), 1037–1050.
McClusky, U. (2005). *To be met as a person. The dynamics of attachment in professional encounters*. Karnac, London.
Mellqvist, G. (2008). Låt känslorna flöda. Moderna chefer skippar pokerfejset. *DIEGO, Dagens Industri*.
Miller, A. (1996). *The drama of the gifted child. The search for the true self* (3rd ed.). Basic Books.
Nathanson, D. L. (1992). *Shame and pride. Affect, sex and birth of the self.* Norton &.
Nesbit, P. L. (2012). The role of self-reflection, emotional management of feedback, and self-regulation processes in self-directed leadership development. *Human Resource Development, 11*(2), 203–226.
Nussbaum, M. C. (2001). *Upheavals of thought. The intelligence of emotions*. Cambridge University Press.
Rajah, R., Song, Z., & Arvey, R. (2011). Emotionality and leadership: Taking stock of the past decade of research. *The Leadership Quarterly, 22*, 1107–1119.
Salovey, P., & Mayer, J. D. (1990). Emotional intelligence. *Imagination, Cognition and Personality, 9*(3), 185–211.
Schermer, V. L. (2018). Four modalities of the experience of others in groups. *Group Analysis, 51*(2), 175–196.
Serrat, O. (2017). Understanding and developing emotional intelligence. In *Knowledge solutions*. Springer.
Simpson, P., & French, R. (2006). Negative capability and the capacity to think in the present moment: Some implications for leadership. *Leadership, 2*(2), 245–255.
Solms, M. (2021). *The hidden spring. A journey to the source of consciousness*. W.W. Norton & Company, Inc..
Stern, D. N. (1985). *The interpersonal world of the infant*. Basic Books.

Stern, D. N. (1995). *The motherhood constellation. A unified view of parent-infant psychotherapy*. Routledge.

Sy, T., Coté, S., & Saavedra, R. (2005). The contagious leader: Impact of the leader's mood on the mood of group members, group affective tone, and group processes. *Journal of Applied Psychology, 90*(2), 295–305.

Tse, H. H. M., Troth, A. C., Ashkanasy, N. M., & Colins, A. T. (2018). Affect and leader-member exchange in the new millennium: A state-of-art review and guiding framework. *The Leadership Quarterly, 29*, 135–149. https://doi.org/10.1016/j.leaqua.2017.10.002

Vingerhoets, A. (2013). *Why only humans weep. Unravelling the mysteries of tears*. Oxford University Press. ISBN 978-0-198-57024-0.

Visser, V. A., van Knippenberg, D., Van Kleef, G. A., & Wisse, B. (2013). How leader displays of happiness and sadness influence follower performance: Emotional contagion and creative versus analytical performance. *The Leadership Quarterly, 24*(1), 172–188.

Weber, M. (1948). *From Max Weber: Essays in sociology*. H. H. Gerth, & C. Wright Mills (Eds.). Routledge.

Why Do We Want to Work?

5

To be used to one's full potential.

Why do people want to work? And why does work arouse so much emotion in people? Before we move on, we must take a closer look at human needs and driving forces, which influence our motivation to work. We must also examine the meaning of work. All these things are intimately associated with our emotional life. Why are we motivated to do some things and not others? Why are we motivated to do anything at all?

It is often proposed that people do not really want to work. Sometimes popular television shows and lifestyle magazines depict work as a necessary evil. As something one simply must put up with and take care of as quickly as possible to make time for everything else that really makes life enjoyable. Does that image match reality? At least it is only one side of the coin. If that was our only motivation, we would need both carrots and whips to work. A decent salary and decent working conditions might be regarded as the carrot, while the whip consists of all sorts of unpleasant sanctions that come into play if tasks are not carried out satisfactory. And it's the boss's job to administer both whip and carrot.

Work has long suffered from this carrot-whip perspective on work motivation. Of course, we must not disregard the fact that human behavior to a large extent is governed by its consequences. However, the carrot and whip metaphor is simplistic and misleading (Pettinger, 2010). A focus on rewards and punishments might also reinforce manipulative behavior in leaders. Such behavior reflects a kind of destructive leadership that has negative consequences for the organization (see Chap. 7). Much research is also critical of the carrot-whip approach to leadership, where managers and co-workers are seen as adversaries with different goals (Arnold & Randall, 2016; Herzberg et al., 2011; Jaques, 1996; Seligman, 2002/2007).

C. Sandahl, M. von Knorring, *Managing with Sense and Sensitivity*, https://doi.org/10.1007/978-3-031-24109-3_5

Of course, there may be some justification for this approach if maximizing shareholders' return and executive compensation are a company's primary goals. If that is the case, only a good salary can motivate the individual. Who feels work commitment if only others are richly rewarded? However, most companies and organizations have larger aims and other agendas than return on investment or solely cost efficiency. They also wish to satisfy the needs of other stakeholders: co-workers, customers, suppliers, and even society. To satisfy these needs, organizations require strong productivity ratios, high-quality goods and services, and a record of sustainable profitability (in for-profit companies) and cost-efficiency (in public organizations). These factors are necessary conditions. However, in today's competitive world, many financial, social, and political factors require maximum flexibility and adaptability at all levels if organizations are to be sustainable. Thus, co-worker collaboration and commitment are required. If your leadership style reflects a belief – even if not expressed or demonstrated openly – that no one really wants to work, it is unlikely a spirit of co-worker collaboration and commitment will develop in your company.

This is not new organizational knowledge. In the 1960s, for example, organization researchers demonstrated that the view that people do not really want to work was at risk of becoming a self-fulfilling prophecy that threatened co-workers' engagement and thereby the companies' productivity. A more productivity friendly view was the opposite. They found that when managers trusted their co-workers and clearly communicated company goals to them, company productivity and co-worker responsibility increased (Argyris, 1982; McGregor, 1960). The employees thus seemed to want to work and take responsibility for the business when they understood the goals and purpose of their work and was treated in a good way.

People have always understood the need to work, because human beings have always been dependent on each other. Human work is simply a prerequisite for human life. We understand from our own and others' experiences that work can be, and often is, very satisfying. Even completion of postponed everyday tasks, such as making the beds or washing the dishes, can be satisfying. If work sometimes feels daunting, we nevertheless feel satisfaction when we have made an effort and performed the task. It may be that the satisfaction we feel when we have done a job is part of our natural survival instinct, which we share with all living things. Work is simply a prerequisite for fulfilled human life.

We think work supports existential human conditions and emotions, such as acknowledgment, community, security, joy, and creativity. In his book, *Escape from Freedom* (1943/1994), Erich Fromm (1900–1980) asserted that people have a fundamental and existential need to contribute positively to society. By creating structures and affirming values that make life better, people also create better conditions for family survival. Work, therefore, gives people the opportunity to create relationships and to develop and exert influence.

Yet it is an exaggeration to think people have no other needs than work. We have many other relational needs derived from instincts, such as playing, seeking, and caring (see Chap. 4), some of which are even work-related.

Needs-Based Human Motivation

Various motivation theories are found in the organization and management literature. A common thread in this literature is the general agreement that people are motivated by a few basic needs. The strength and type of human needs vary – person-to-person and life stage-to-life stage. However, considering how basic and vital needs are, it is not surprising that the workplace becomes an arena, where many emotions are expressed. For you as a manager to gain a greater understanding of the driving forces behind yours and others' actions, we will give a brief description of these human basic needs.

The Need for Nearness, Acknowledgment, and Safety

For a long time, it was believed that human needs could be ranked in a hierarchy with the most fundamental needs – food, water, warmth, and rest – at the base of this hierarchical pyramid. This assumption was based on the theory developed by the influential American psychologist Abraham Maslow (1908–1970). He ranked other needs in ascending order in the pyramid: safety and security, human relationships, prestige and the sense of accomplishment, and self-fulfillment (Maslow, 1954). He theorized that people could not satisfy these psychological needs until their physiological needs were satisfied. This theory had considerable influence in society, and still has. However, other researchers have found that needs cannot be ranked in this way. Here, we describe how human relationships in some situations even trump physiological needs.

After World War II, many European children whose parents were missing or had died were placed in orphanages. Caretakers found that many of these children, whose basic needs were well provided for, suffered from depression and fainting spells. Some children died, although they had no diseases or illnesses and had received nutritious food, clean clothes, and warm beds. The World Health Organization (WHO) commissioned the psychiatrist and psychoanalyst John Bowlby (1907–1990) to investigate this situation. He discovered the children lacked an essential biological need – nearness to a small number of adults. According to Bowlby, clean clothes and nourishment cannot wholly substitute for close human relationships (Bowlby, 1988).

It is only in recent decades that attachment theory (McClusky, 2005) has become widely accepted. According to this theory, infants cannot survive without physical contact with another human being. People, from birth, are instinctively drawn to an adult protector. This phenomenon is observable by the eye contact that even infants seek.

Physical proximity, eye contact, and touch communicate the security and safety that everyone, child and adult alike, requires in life. The child's expectation of security and safety can be distorted and disturbed, if the child is repeatedly rejected, criticized, betrayed, or simply ignored. Such treatment can have traumatic consequences for children and for those around them. Severe depression and other signs of emotional trauma, including violence, are not uncommon in such children.

Reactions to such treatment among adults are seldom that dramatic in the workplace. However, all humans rely on a safe social context to survive and thrive (Edmondson, 2018). Feelings of isolation or loneliness will increase vigilance for threat and feelings of vulnerability. When this happens, it will influence physiological functioning and affect, for example, sleep pattern, and even increase morbidity and mortality (Hawkley & Cacioppo, 2010). Co-workers who are emotionally distanced by the aloofness of their managers may find the workplace an unsafe and insecure environment, which will affect them emotionally and increase stress levels.

People who are on long-term sick leave because of fatigue, depression, or overwork describe their vulnerability in the workplace. Typically, they say their managers or co-workers did not support them or betrayed their trust. These people tend to conceal their depression. For various reasons, they suppress what they consider very legitimate feelings of disappointment, anger, and resentment.

While it may sometimes be difficult to reconcile people's need for human contact, affirmation, and security with the image of people as independent individualists, people may exhibit both behavior patterns of dependency and independency. We must recognize people's inherent need to explore, create, and develop, sometimes independently on one's own and at other times together with mates – without these inspirations, human life will not advance. These needs, for human contact, security, exploration, and creation, are deeply seated in the human biology and must be considered at work.

Other Human Needs

To this point, we have discussed the needs for nearness, acknowledgment, and safety and the need to create, explore, and develop. Later in the chapter, we will examine the need for life balance and the existential need of experiencing and creating meaning. These needs are highly relevant in discussions of work. But human needs are of course not limited to these. Three more needs are usually highlighted in theories on motivation (Lichtenberg, 1989).

The first of these concerns physiological needs, such as food, drink, and rest, which are, of course, necessary for our survival. In today's seemingly never-ending work life, however, sometimes managers and co-workers ignore or at least temporarily forget about these needs. As an example, suddenly you realize the lunch break is over, and you have not eaten. Or maybe you wake at three in the morning and begin to rewrite today's presentation. Or you receive an urgent, reply-requested, email from your boss while you are on vacation. Many people today agree that work seems endless.

The second category refers to the need for self-protection and the necessity for self-defense. We protect ourselves by aggression (fight) or avoidance (flight). This is not primarily a matter of congenital aggression or avoidance; it is the need for a basic survival system when confronted with danger of some kind.

Finally, sensual pleasure and sexual arousal are needs that are usually described as fundamental to the human condition.

All these needs can have profound social consequences, because of their complex role in personal relationships and sometimes even in work relationships. When these needs are frustrated, or cannot find an adequate expression, emotions more than reason may be activated. In positive situations, when one does not get stuck in the emotional side of the frustration, it can stimulate problem-solving and creative thinking. For example, a well-functioning working group, who feels their survival threatened, can put great commitment on creating new working methods that can streamline operations.

Needs and motivation are closely related in the sense that needs drives and direct motivation. If basic needs are not sufficiently well satisfied, the engagement and motivation for work will be limited. As managers, we need to be able to recognize when there is such an imbalance in our co-workers' work life and in our own life.

The Biological Basis for Motivation

In Chap. 4, we described the biological basis of human *emotions*. To further explore how emotions and needs affect work, we will take a closer look at the concept of motivation – in this chapter with respect to the biological basis of *motivation* and what the implications are for healthy work.

According to *neurobiology*, the following three basic motivational systems exist, of which the first two below are reward systems (Sapolsky, 2017):

1. The *exploratory* system (related to the hormone dopamine) is characterized by interest, curiosity, and enthusiasm. Ideally, we, of course, want co-workers to a large extent to be motivated by this system.
2. The *security* system (related to oxytocin and endorphins) is characterized by responses, such as joy, peace, reflection, and creativity. It is also characteristic for individuals who are part of well-functioning work groups (see Chap. 6).
3. The *threat* system (related to adrenalin and cortisol) is characterized by responses such as fight, flight, and freeze. When the threat system dominates, it is a sign of an ill-functioning work group where co-workers do not feel safe.

In all mammals, including human beings, the exploratory system is active, unless the other two take over. Unfortunately, the threat system is three to four times more sensitive than the reward systems. However, from a survival and evolutionary perspective, this increased sensitivity is not necessarily a liability. However, from a manager's perspective, it is sometimes frustrating to find that small, well-intended changes to the workplace or the organization sometimes result in strong negative emotions, because of the easily activated threat system.

Which then are the social factors that trigger these sensitive biological threat and reward systems? There are several ways to categorize social cues that humans are sensitive to. We have chosen to briefly refer to a model developed by David Rock, a physician and cofounder of the Neuro Leadership Institute in New York, and his coauthor, Christine Cox. They identified five domains of experience the brain's threat and rewards systems respond to (Rock & Cox, 2012). They are the following: status, certainty, autonomy, relatedness, and fairness (SCARF). Probably these factors are familiar to anyone involved in work environment issues, even if they never have heard about exactly this model. Perhaps less well-known is that neuroscience research has confirmed that these domains are essential for the survival and development of human beings as biological creatures.

Rock and Cox (2012) argue that we need to understand how the social cues in these five domains activate our threat system, to be better prepared to avoid these cues in the workplace. Even better, we can learn how to substitute threatening social cues with rewarding social cues that stimulate exploration and security – an activity that can lead to greater work interest, engagement, and satisfaction among our co-workers. How can we make that substitution? Rock and Cox (2012) suggested that we simply replace the threatening social cues with rewarding social cues, i.e.:

1. Create clarity about *status* and roles.
2. Provide *certainty* including a safe workplace, physically, and psychologically.
3. Encourage co-worker *autonomy*.
4. Encourage *relatedness*.
5. Be *fair*.

The SCARF model corresponds well with the often-cited self-determination theory (SDT) on human motivation, development, and wellness described by Deci et al. (2017), who concluded that co-workers have three basic psychological needs: *autonomy*, *relatedness,* and *competence.* In Chap. 6, we will develop this topic further in relation to the concept *psychological safety* (Edmondson, 2018).

The Importance of Life Balance

One reason why we address the basic needs and conditions of human life in a book for managers is that many people spend a lot of time and energy at work, sometimes at the cost of rest and recovery. One prerequisite for work is life balance. There is always a risk that work dominates life to such an extent that other areas of life are neglected. This can be observed as a modern human phenomenon: the increase in the number of people who spend so much time and energy on work that they have difficulty doing other things, including satisfying their basic human needs. In today's often boundaryless work environment, it is easy to slip into such a pattern (Palm et al., 2020). The results often include unhealthy eating habits, poor sleep patterns, and a failure to set aside enough time for nourishment and sleep. This work-life imbalance can have negative consequences in many areas of life, including work, decision-making, and ethical reflection.

In ancient times, the concepts of the active life (*vita activa*), the contemplative life (*vita contemplativa*), and the regenerative life (*vita regenerativa*) referred to three aspects of the human condition. To lead a healthy physical and mental life, people need to achieve a sensible balance among these three ways of living. The German American philosopher Hannah Arendt (1906–1975) linked these concepts in perhaps her most well-known book, *The Human Condition* (1958/2018). According to Arendt, the active life refers to people's engagement with political and economic institutions. The contemplative life refers to human thinking, will, judgment, and reflection. The regenerative life refers to rest, sleep, and recovery. Ideally, in Arendt's view, life balance requires spending a third of every day in each of the three "lives."

The ideal of a life in balance as described by Arendt might be very hard to live up to in the realities of modern life. Often, there is a combined pressure from work and family, sometimes including obligations and demands in relation to children and/or ageing parents. After periods of intense work, the brain needs time to rest. Sleep is of course the most important form of recovery, but psychical activity or enjoying relaxing social encounters are as important. Or you might want to, as Arendt suggests, just find time for yourself.

Another aspect related to a life in balance and recovery from stress is the research evidence for the positive impact of *nature* on mental and physical health (Annerstedt van den Bosch et al., 2016; Lottrup et al., 2012). The human eye distinguishes *green* more clearly than any other color. On the African savanna, this visual trait can provide a survival advantage, which explains the evolutionary background to our need for greenery. Exposure to nature, including green infrastructures, has been shown to increase life expectancy, decrease physical and psychological health risks, reduce stress levels, help recover concentration, motivate physical activity, increase work capacity, and promote greater job satisfaction (Stoltz & Grahn, 2021). Green spaces, according to these researchers, help people at work recover from stressful events or situations – so don't underestimate a walk in the park. It can also provide time and space for reflection.

When Needs Are Frustrated

One message in this book is that work itself is not the cause of injury or illness – excluding, for example, injuries from dangerous physical work or illnesses from hazardous chemical exposure. Nevertheless, people can become ill from the emotions aroused when they are unable to work in a productive or satisfying way. It is sometimes claimed that work is the adult's equivalent of child play. Like play, work is often enjoyable. For some people, work enjoyment – like play – derives from the social cooperation that work often requires. Yet, in addition to such pleasure, work – like play – may lead to disappointment, conflict, and rivalry. In such cases, people may lose interest in their work. Anger, grief, shame, and guilt are common emotional responses when the work is no longer fun. Unfortunately, this happens much too often in the workplace.

Often a sense of not being able to use one's competence, lies behind the frustration experienced in the workplace. In such situations, the biological threat system becomes activated. Co-workers may then respond with doubt, bitterness, and hostility in ways that disrupt their work-life balance and create distrust. In such wary situations, it can be difficult to know how to get out of the locked situation. Then, plenty of time is needed for reflection, and sometimes even consultation with outsiders, including social interaction with friends and relatives. Such reflection can offer some distance and lead to a change of perspective, which in turn might open for alternative coping strategies.

The German American philosopher Paul Tillich (1886–1965) thought that unsatisfied existential, psychological, and social needs can easily provoke strong emotional responses (Tillich, 1952/2014). He further claimed that it may be difficult to understand the origin of these responses – one's own and those of others. For example, one person may refuse the management assignment of a prestigious project, because the project's purpose is counter to an inner conviction. Another person may resist the same assignment, because it is so complex that the project may lead to physical and mental exhaustion and emotional hypersensitivity. A third person may simply accept the assignment with indifference, with no thoughts or feelings about its complexity or purpose. It is easy as a manager to fall into the trap of believing that one's own way of being and reacting is the norm for everybody else and to forget that people are different.

Mental Exhaustion and Occupational Burnout

Mental exhaustion and occupational burnout are reactions to long-term stress, including an overload of work, high demands, lack of control, or limited decision latitude (Theorell & Karasek, 1996). Mental exhaustion may also result when people find no meaning in life. They are then unable to balance life's various demands and pressures. People may also feel mentally exhausted when their human momentum is restrained, such that they are unable to use their natural abilities or to think rationally in a meaningful way. The same can occur when the biological threat system becomes activated under long periods, because of lack of clear roles, uncertain status, insecurity, lack of autonomy, exclusion, or injustice (according to the SCARF model above, also described in more detail in Chap. 6). The resulting frustration and demotivation can cause human suffering as well as the waste of company and societal resources (Lohela-Karlsson et al., 2015).

Deficient organizational and social work environments have been linked to the increase in mental illness. In a study conducted in the EU, Leka et al. (2015) estimated that between 50% and 60% of sick leave is attributable to work-related stress. In Sweden, for example, work-related depression, mainly due to occupational burnout and other stress-related diagnoses, is increasingly listed as a cause of sick leave (Social Insurance Report, 2020: 8). Similar developments have been observed in many other countries. Recent statistics support the conclusion that this relationship is a globally important issue with huge economic consequences (Hewlett & Moran, 2014; OECD, 2012, 2021).

People who ignore or lose touch with their own needs, motivations, and core values (including work meaningfulness) often experience depression-like symptoms, including mental exhaustion and disengagement from work. This condition is sometimes labeled exhaustion syndrome, which is the clinical and psychiatric equivalent of occupational burnout. The label clearly describes the actual condition: exhaustion that cannot be successfully treated with rest. Symptoms involve concentration and memory difficulties, physical fatigue, lack of staying power, problems with recuperating and sleeping, hypersensitivity, negative reactions to demands, and irritability (Besér et al., 2014).

Numerous cases of people with occupational burnout have been identified. These cases often describe individuals who are so committed to their work that they are shocked when work suddenly seems meaningless. The explanations may be multiple. One explanation may relate to people's need to belong. When people feel safe among those they work with (i.e., the attachment system is in balance), they can achieve a favorable balance between reason and emotion that leads to successful problem focus, analysis, and resolution. When this balance is disturbed, the ability to work is also undermined (Demerouti et al., 2001).

Occupational burnout may also be caused by having to work in ways that violate one's moral convictions. The concept of moral distress, which originated in 1984 (Jameton, 1984, 1993), has since been explored in many scientific articles (e.g., McCarthy & Gastmans, 2015; Musto & Rodney, 2016). Moral distress can arise, for example, when nurses or physicians lack the resources, competences, and support needed to provide the quality healthcare their professional ethics require. These deficiencies, if they persist over time, can cause excessive workload, erosion of professional pride, and a sense of helplessness. Work may lose its meaning and purpose.

It is true, however, that our needs are never completely satisfied – nor should they be. It is conceivable that this dissatisfaction drives us to tackle new challenges and to set new goals, alone or with others. It is perhaps our longing for fulfillment that urges us forward – sometimes to the point of exhaustion. The paradox is that we are encouraged to accept ourselves, and, at the same time, we are encouraged to develop our full potential. We can always do more, always become better.

As a manager you must balance needs and driving forces, your own and the co-workers. On the one hand, you need to calmly accept the need for rest and tranquility; on the other hand, you need to promote your own and others need for development and progress. We reemphasize that exploration of new experiences, competence, and mastery are fundamental human needs. For various reasons, these needs may sometimes be frustrated. Nevertheless, as a manager, you should realize that development cannot be forced, only gently supported and acknowledged. In Chap. 7, we return to this discussion.

Experiencing and Creating Meaning

As stated above, one prerequisite for wanting to work and for taking satisfaction in work is that work must be meaningful to those who perform it. Still, for many people in the world, work equates with survival. On the other hand, an increasing number of people are in sufficiently stable and secure socioeconomic situations that work does not compare solely with survival. Their work must also be meaningful in other ways. Meaningfulness, in the sense of a quality that gives life importance and value, is a basic need in most theories on human motivation, including for people in less fortunate circumstances.

Creating meaning in one's life involves exploration and mastery of new experiences and skills. Creating meaning also involves spiritual or existential motivation when people seek relationships with other people, nature, society, and perhaps God. All major religions – Buddhism, Hinduism, Confucianism, Islam, Judaism, and Christianity – have as a fundamental tenet the same ethical principle: concern for others. In work, our concern for others means we create value not only for ourselves but also for others.

Aaron Antonovsky (1923–1994), an Israeli American researcher in medical sociology, analyzed meaning and context in life and work (Antonovsky, 1987). He coined the term "sense of coherence" (SOC) to describe how the experiences of comprehensibility, manageability, and meaningfulness affect our health. Viktor Frankl (1905–1997), the Austrian psychiatrist and philosopher, examined meaning in several books as a necessity for human health and well-being. He writes in his book, *The Will to Meaning* (1969/2014), that our entire existence is at risk if we lack a strong idea or ideal to cling to. Elliott Jaques (1917–2003), the Canadian psychoanalyst and organizational theorist, argued that people need to feel their work matters to at least one other person (Jaques, 1996). Like Antonovsky, Jaques concluded that meaning was important as a work motivator and for physical and mental health. He also argued that work must be demanding in the sense that decisions require some effort. Then, it contributes to an experience of being competent. The kind of decisions that require an effort is of course different between people. What is easy for one is too demanding for somebody else.

From this examination of the meaning of work, we may conclude that work does not derive its meaning solely from the economic value of the goods or services that organizations produce. Rather, the meaning of work derives from its importance to people and society. As an example, consider an apartment building in which the tenants agree to upgrade the garden in the shared courtyard. They clean, rake, and plant bulbs and perennials. Everyone is very pleased with the result. Possibly some economic value has been created, at least for the building's owners. For the tenants, however, value derives from the successful completion of their beautification project. Value from their perspective does not equate with the project's economic value.

Or consider the joy we experience from a child's or grandchild's drawings or music recital. Or recall our pleasure provoked by the subway barrier guard's friendliness as he greets commuters every morning. Life is about much more than regular meals and warm homes. We are social beings who require security, protection, and others' devotion and loyalty. At work, we depend in large degree on others for this support.

Johansson et al. (2011) studied a healthcare clinic that received Sweden's annual "best workplace" award. They found that co-worker job satisfaction was the main reason the healthcare clinic received the award. The co-workers were proud of the high standard of their work, which was deeply meaningful and significant for their patients. The second reason was the managers' consistent leadership style – that is, the managers lived by the values they espoused. Furthermore, the co-workers were autonomous and allowed to make decisions independently. They also worked harmoniously as a group; people readily pitched in whenever extra hands were needed. Last, but not least, the managers and co-workers all felt that they realized their vision of providing high-quality healthcare. The award was well-deserved.

What motivates people to do meaningful and important work like the work at the healthcare clinic described above? Is it altruism or egoism or perhaps both? It is often assumed that altruists place others' well-being before their own interests while egoists prioritize their own interests (Rachels, 2009). However, we may also understand human motivation as both altruistic and egoistic. We do not mean that people are altruistic (i.e., selfless) for selfish reasons such that they are merely instruments for personal benefit. In many instances, people support others' interests because of their general benevolence toward others. Nowak (2006) regards this capacity for reciprocity and altruism as a decisive factor for mankind's societal development. Another interpretation of "the selfish motivation," however, is self-preservation. In this theory, people act selflessly, because they recognize in others the same human dignity that they themselves possess.

References

Annerstedt van den Bosch, M., Mudu, P., Uscila, V., Barrdahl, M., Kulinkina, A., Staatsen, B., et al. (2016). Development of an urban green space indicator and the public health rationale. *Scandinavian Journal of Public Health, 44*(2), 159–167.

Antonovsky, A. (1987). *Unraveling the mystery of health: How people manage stress and stay well*. Jossey-Bass.

Arendt, H. (1958/2018). *The human condition*. University of Chicago Press.

Argyris, C. (1982). *Learning and action: Individual and organizational*. Jossey-Bass.

Arnold, J., & Randall, R. (2016). *Work psychology. Understanding human behavior in the workplace*. FT Publishing Int.

Beseŕ, A., Sorjonen, K., Wahlberg, K., Peterson, U., Nygren, Å., & Åsberg, M. (2014). Construction and evaluation of a self-rating scale for stress-induced exhaustion disorder, the Karolinska Exhaustion Disorder Scale. *Scandinavian Journal of Psychology, 55*, 72–82.

Bowlby, J. (1988). *A secure base*. Routledge.

Deci, E. L., Olafsen, A. H., & Ryan, R. M. (2017). Self-determination theory in work organizations: The state of a science. *Annual Review of Organizational Psychology and Organizational Behavior, 4*, 19–43.

Demerouti, E., Bakker, A. B., de Jonge, J., Janssen, P. P. M., & Schaufeli, W. B. (2001). Burnout and engagement at work as a function of demands and control. *Scandinavian Journal of Work, Environment & Health, 4*, 279–286.

Edmondson, A. C. (2018). *The fearless organization. Creating psychological safety in the workplace for learning, innovation and growth.* Wiley.
Frankl, V. E. (1969/2014). *The will to meaning. Foundations and applications of logotherapy.* Penguin Putnam. ISBN 9780142181263.
Fromm, E. (1943/1994). *Escape from freedom.* Henry Holt Company.
Hawkley, L. C., & Cacioppo, J. T. (2010). Loneliness matters: A theoretical and empirical review of consequences and mechanisms. *Annals of Behavioral Medicine, 40*(2), 218–227.
Herzberg, F., Mausner, B., & Bloch Snyderman, B. (2011). *The motivation to work. E-book.* Transaction Publisher.
Hewlett, E., & Moran, V. (2014). *Making mental health count: The social and economic costs of neglecting mental health care*. OECD.
Jameton, A. (1984). *Nursing practice: The ethical issues*. Prentice-Hall.
Jameton, A. (1993). Dilemmas of moral distress: Moral responsibility and nursing practice. *Clinical Issues in Perinatal and Women's Health Nursing, 4*(4), 542–551.
Jaques, E. (1996). *Requisite organization. A total system for effective managerial organization and managerial leadership for the 21st century.* Cason Hall.
Johansson, G., Sandahl, C., & Andershed, B. (2011). Authentic and congruent leadership providing excellent work environment in palliative care. *Leadership in Health Services, 24*(2), 135–149.
Leka, S., Jain, A., Iavicoli, S., & Di Tecco, C. (2015). An evaluation of the policy context on psychosocial risks and mental health in the workplace in the European Union: Achievements, challenges, and the future. *BioMed Research International, 2015*, 213089. https://doi.org/10.1155/2015/213089
Lichtenberg, J. (1989). *Psychoanalysis and motivation.* The Analytic Press.
Lohela-Karlsson, M., Hagberg, J., & Bergström, G. (2015). Production loss among employees perceiving work environment problems. *International Archives of Occupational and Environmental Health, 88*, 769–777.
Lottrup, L., Stigsdotter, U. K., Meilby, H., & Corazon, S. S. (2012). Associations between use, activities and characteristics of the outdoor environment at workplaces. *Urban Forestry & Urban Greening, 11*(2), 159–168.
Maslow, A. H. (1954). *Motivation and personality*. Harper.
McCarthy, J., & Gastmas, C. (2015). Moral distress. A review of the argument-based nursing ethics literature. *Nursing Ethics, 22*(1), 131–152.
McCluskey, U. (2005). *To be met as a person: The dynamics of attachment in professional encounters*. Routledge.
McGregor, D. (1960). *The human side of enterprise*. McGraw Hill.
Musto, L. C., & Rodney, P. A. (2016). Moving from conceptual ambiguity to knowledgeable action: Using a critical realist approach to studying moral distress. *Nursing Philosophy, 17*, 75–87.
Nowak, M. A. (2006). Five rules for the evolution of cooperation. *Science, 314*(5805), 1560–1563.
OECD. (2012). *Sick on the job? Myths and realities about mental health and work* (Mental health and work). OECD Publishing.
OECD. (2021). *Fitter minds, fitter jobs: From awareness to change in integrated mental health, skills and work policies* (Mental health and work). OECD Publishing.
Palm, K., Bergman, A., & Rosengren, C. (2020). Towards more proactive sustainable human resource management practices? A study on stress due to the ICT-mediated integration of work and private life. *Sustainability, 12*(20), 8303.
Pettinger, R. (2010). *Organizational behaviour. Performance management in practice*. Routledge. ISBN 9780415481434.
Rachels, S. (2009). *The elements of moral philosophy*. McGraw-Hill.
Rock, D., & Cox, C. (2012). SCARF in 2012: Updating the social neuroscience of collaborating with others. *Neuro Leadership journal, 4*(4), 1–16.
Sapolsky, R. M. (2017). *Behave: The biology of humans at our best and worst*. Penguin.
Seligman, M. E. P. (2002/2007). *Authentic happiness: Using the new positive psychology to realize your potential for lasting fulfillment*. Free Press.

Social Insurance Report. (2020). *Sjukfrånvaro i psykiatriska diagnoser – En registerstudie av Sveriges arbetande befolkning i åldern 20–69 år* (Sick leave due to psychiatric diagnoses). Socialförsäkringsrapport 2020: 8. ISSN 1654–8574, Försäkringskassan.

Stoltz, J., & Grahn, P. (2021). Perceived sensory dimensions: An evidence-based approach to greenspace aesthetics. *Urban Forestry & Urban Greening, 59*, 126989.

Theorell, T., & Karasek, R. A. (1996). Current issues relating to psychosocial job strain and cardiovascular disease research. *Journal of Occupational Health Psychology, 1*(1), 9–26. (Retraction published 1995, Stress Medicine, 11[1], 17–26).

Tillich, P. (1952/2014). *The courage to be* (3rd ed.). Yale University Press.

Group Dynamics

6

As a manager, you are a member of your group.

The work group, with its own dynamics and development stages, is an often-overlooked element in the organizational psychology literature and in the management literature. As a manager, you need to understand how emotions and reason interact in groups and how this interaction influences your efforts to improve the organization's performance.

As a manager, you have a relationship not only with your individual co-workers, one by one, but also with an entire group of people. You are also a member of that group. Even if you must remain partially distant from the social interactions of the others, you cannot stand totally apart from the group as an observer. Standing at the boundary of a group, inside and outside at the same time, requires skill. It is an intricate balancing act that some managers find quite stressful. Nevertheless, the relationship is intrinsic to the managerial role.

Managers influence the group in various ways, although they are not always aware of the extent of their influence. Managers even contribute to the group dynamics with their silence and their passivity. Managers cannot "not communicate," as has often been remarked.

However, the group members also draw boundaries around their managers' actions. Leadership, as discussed in Chap. 3, is thus a function not only of the individual manager's ways of being as a leader but also of the group dynamics. In large measure, leadership and group dynamics are two sides of the same coin. Leadership is clearly impossible without the group.

Before we examine the managerial role, we need to examine how groups work. That is, we need to understand group dynamics. To investigate these dynamics as a phenomenon, we begin by describing the concept of the group. To help us understand how work groups function optimally, we turn to the field of group psychology.

C. Sandahl, M. von Knorring, *Managing with Sense and Sensitivity*,
https://doi.org/10.1007/978-3-031-24109-3_6

What Is the Group?

An organization consists of people who interact in different constellations – in groups – for the purpose of achieving some end. The group may take various forms: project groups, permanent or temporary teams, management groups, units, departments, divisions, and so on. Some groups may form spontaneously to solve ad hoc problems. Such groups are usually temporary in duration. Other groups to work on complex problems or issues that are expected to require continued attention are also formed. These groups, which have permanent or semipermanent status in the organization, are usually led by a middle manager, a supervisor, or a project manager.

Leadership and management researchers sometimes distinguish among three types of work groups: crews, project groups, and teams. Team is the broader concept, which we will return to further down, but let us start with the two other categories. Crews and project groups can be regarded as team subcategories. Thus, a crew can be seen as an action team and a project group as a development team. In crews, people work together for a specific period (usually measured in hours or days) and in a specific context (often safety-related). Crew members, who usually have clearly defined roles, often identify more with their profession than with the crew itself. Crew protocols typically specify member tasks, work routines, and the use of checklists. Airplane flight crews, incident response teams, operating room teams, emergency teams, and intensive care unit teams are examples of crews.

In project groups, people also work together for a specific time period (usually measured in weeks or months). Their purpose is to complete a particular project following a project schedule. Project groups are often multidisciplinary. Typical examples of project groups are product-, service-, or safety-development groups.

What Is a Team?

Normally teams differ from crews or project groups in that they are longer-lived. The composition of teams changes as old members leave and new members join. Typical examples of teams are production, service, and management teams.

However, an increasingly popular trend in contemporary organizations is to organize the work in teams. Such teams, which may form and dissolve frequently, are often spread across different sites. Employees are frequently assigned to more than one team, and sometimes they disband quickly (Edmondson, 2012; Söderhjelm, 2018). Therefore, we need to pay attention to the process of teaming, i.e., look at it as a dynamic activity rather than only analyzing team as a noun. How can it be learned? Which are the skills that must be developed? How can one shift roles between different teams? How can teaming be facilitated (Edmondson, 2012; Sundlin et al., 2022)? We will return to this topic later in this chapter. However, we believe that is also important to look at the characteristics of a well-functioning team.

In the literature, one can find several definitions of *team*. Kozlowski and Ilgen (2006), argue that a team consists of at least two persons with a common goal in the context of relevant tasks for the organization. The team members interact, and the goals of their work, the workflow, and its outcome demand an interdependency even though the team members have different roles and responsibilities.

The American psychologist, Richard Hackman (2002), contributed to work group psychology with his differentiation between real teams and pseudo teams. In a *pseudo team*, although members report that they belong to a team, they may have only the same manager and/or share the same work site. They do not depend on each other to complete their tasks.

A *real team* is characterized by the following (Hackman, 2002):

- A shared and clearly defined goal.
- The tasks require the members to work together rather than alone or in parallel.
- There is a stability in the group composition.
- All members know who the other members are.
- The individual roles, including the role of the leader, are understood and accepted by everyone.
- The members' skills, social norms, and behaviors must be suitable for tasks and compatible with those of the other members.
- Regularly scheduled team meetings are held in which the team's goals and tasks are evaluated, discussed, and modified as needed.

Others have arrived at similar descriptions. Woods and West (2019) highlighted clarity and shared understanding of goals and roles, the interdependence between team members, and the importance of reflexivity, i.e., to set aside time for evaluation and improvement. The Google Project Aristotle on team effectiveness summarized its findings in five factors:

1. *Psychological safety*: Can we take risks on this team without feeling insecure or embarrassed?
2. *Dependability*: Can we count on each other to do high quality work on time?
3. *Structure and clarity*: Are goals, roles, and execution plans on our team clear?
4. *Meaning of work*: Are we working on something that is personally important for each of us?
5. *Impact of work:* Do we fundamentally believe that the work we're doing matters? (Rozovsky, 2015, p. 1).

The author of this report argued that the first factor, psychological safety, was by far the most important one of the five key factors. We will return to this concept later in this chapter.

As the research reveals, members in well-functioning work groups or real teams generally demonstrate more job satisfaction, greater productivity, and better work quality than individuals working alone. They also have lower stress levels and better health (Edmondson, 2018; Jacobsson et al., 2014; Salas et al., 2013; Wheelan,

2005b; Woods & West, 2019). For example, a study conducted at 147 English hospitals found that those where "real team membership" characteristics dominated, compared to hospitals with "coacting group membership" as the typical, had increased patient safety and reduced patient mortality and experienced fewer employee sick leave absences and lower rates of staff turnover (Lyubovnikova et al., 2015).

Online Groups

During the Covid-19 pandemic in the early 2020s, organizations significantly increased their use of online groups. Many employees had to develop the skills needed to arrange, conduct, and participate in online meetings. The many advantages of such groups include flexibility, speed, and easy accessibility. Online groups, nevertheless, require the same clarity in task design, task focus, leadership, organizational support, and resource procurement as traditional, in person groups.

However, several disadvantages are associated with online groups. Perhaps one of the most discussed disadvantages is the lack of interpersonal contact when members cannot make eye contact or read others' emotional responses. Misunderstandings are frequent, conflicts arise easily, and poor decision-making increases. Some participants have even pointed to the loss of organizational citizenship that they have experienced in online groups (Woods & West, 2019).

Participating in online groups often means employees must make rapid shifts between meetings and sometimes even work roles. While such shifts can be stressful, they may also be stimulating if there is clarity about the purpose of online meetings and one's role in them. Employees require adequate time to switch between different roles and to reflect on the process and outcomes of online meetings to reduce the stress associated with this way of meeting (Sundlin et al., 2022).

Most principles that apply to groups in which people meet face-to-face seem to apply to online groups. However, because online meetings decrease the members' opportunities to pick up emotional cues, these meetings are limited as long-term solutions, where participant interaction is needed or desirable. Yet, online meetings will continue to be part of work life also in the future. As the same basic meeting dynamics apply to online groups as to in person meetings, here we will describe in person group dynamics research here.

Group Size: Is It Important?

The optimal group size, which depends on many factors, varies with the situation. What is certain is that mankind has formed groups since people began living in primitive communal systems. Anthropologists assume human beings originally formed semi-large or medium size groups (15–40 members). In contrast, today's nuclear family is a small group. Researchers who study group psychology generally conclude that well-functioning groups should have no more than twelve members which not too many decades ago was the average family size in Western cultures.

The American group researcher, Susan Wheelan (1963–2019), studied the importance of group size. In a study of 329 groups with varying tasks, she found that groups with 3–6 members were more productive and advanced than larger groups (Wheelan, 2009). She concluded, in line with Hackman (2002), that work groups should consist of only the members needed to achieve the group's goals. The implication is that work teams as a rule should be as small as possible, usually no bigger than six to eight members. However, there are exceptions. If well-conceived and well-planned, it is possible to build well-functioning teams with 12–15 members.

However, not all work is done in teams. Many examples of work can be found in industry and in the public sector where employees work, relatively independently, in parallel on similar tasks. Sometimes the tasks are complex such as elder care of people in their homes; other tasks are more repetitive such as assembly line work. The control span (i.e., the number of employees one individual can supervise) is larger when the tasks have a simpler nature.

It is not uncommon for managers to supervise quite large groups, sometimes as many as 60–80 people. The group dynamics of large groups are different and less predictable than in small groups (Wilke, 2014). Therefore, large group composition seems more appropriate for simpler tasks.

The optimal number of members in a group also depends on the communication systems available. Because all group members require good information, they also require good communication relationships with other members. As group size increases, effective communication becomes more challenging. The large and largest groups are usually subdivided into medium or small groups because work coordination takes too much time in larger groups. Individual identity, job satisfaction, and cooperation tend to decrease in the large and largest groups compared to that in the medium and small groups (Levine & Moreland, 1990).

In the subgroups, effective communication systems between units and levels are essential (Sundlin & Sundlin, 2014). One way to improve the flow of communication is to assign the communication activities to a member or a work group (i.e., the boundary spanners) who can manage "the spaces" across the organizational boundaries (Alvinius et al., 2016).

Communication is easier, however, if group members visualize the group as a whole – not as a collection of individuals but as a system that has identity and meaning. When people in a group think in terms of systems, the exact number of group members becomes less important (Agazarian et al., 2021).

The small group has many advantages. For example, it is sometimes possible to structure an organization so that managers at every level can form work groups of 3–12 members. Given our knowledge of group dynamics, such organizations will likely have more functional work groups than work groups of more than twelve members – as is often the case today. We conclude that group size is indeed important.

The Individual Versus the Person in Groups

To understand the concept of the group, we need to understand the difference between two other concepts: the individual and the person. In everyday usage, we probably do not notice the difference between them as we write and speak. Nevertheless, a tension exists in their usage because of how people think about themselves and how they relate to others. Simply stated, many people fight a tug-of-war between dependence and independence. This conflict appears in individual human relationships and in groups.

The "individual" refers to the complete and indivisible human being. In a psychological frame of reference, individuality is the basis of human identity, the core of oneself – that is, the perception of who one really is as a separate, self-sufficient, and independent being. If the "individualistic" perspective is taken, one can agree with and work with others but have no compulsion to do so. Nor is it necessary to spend time reflecting on how much one should care about others.

If the individualistic perspective is taken, one may feel trapped as a member of an organization. Then, work exists to satisfy one's private needs and interests rather than to accomplish the organization's purpose (see Chap. 8). In this perspective, the organization exists for me, not the other way around. At this point, organizational life seems too rigid and bureaucratic. Organizations seem to get in the way of one's own self-realization.

The "person" has a different meaning. A person is a conscious, self-reflective, and verbal human being who acts in a historical, social, and physical context. A person's actions, which are dependent on context, are influenced by others' actions. The group psychologist, S. H. Foulkes, used the term matrix, in the sense of uterus or mold, to describe how the person is a node in and dependent on a network of communications with others (Sandahl et al., 2021). As a person, you can represent others, understand how you influence them, and acknowledge how they affect you.

The "person system," which is related to group belonging, seems to be deeply rooted in human biology as social neurobiology, a rapidly increasing research field, proposes. For example, Lieberman (2014) conducted a research project in which the threat to social connectedness was studied using functional brain imaging. One of his experiments included a simple play situation, where the subjects were excluded from the game. When thus excluded, the subjects' brain images revealed activity in the part of the brain known to be activated by physical pain. Furthermore, when the subjects were given a painkiller (paracetamol), the activity in the "pain center" decreased. Lieberman found that the brain experiences social pain and physical pain similarly. The conclusion was that the parts of the brain that are associated with social activities are in constant readiness. Human's sensitivity to social signals, which therefore must be extremely sophisticated, has been compared with the well-developed and sensitive olfactory organs in dogs.

These concepts, individual and person, are not mutually exclusive. They can be used to refer to parallel processes and situations in everyone's life. It is also possible to conclude that the experience of being an individual is the basis for becoming a person in a lifelong process of becoming. In everyday life, including work life, people require self-insight as individuals and as persons. A person who is in a group, where goals can only be achieved by joint efforts and mutual dependence, must consider whether this group work fulfills the potential of oneself as an individual.

The Group as a Whole

A leading figure in social psychology, Kurt Lewin (1890–1947), said that a group forms when group members become mutually dependent on each other (e.g., when their task is to solve a problem or achieve a goal together). A classic example of a group is the following: a crowd waits for a bus. They pay no attention to others. When two cars crash into each other close to the bus stop, some in the crowd help passengers out of the cars while others call for an ambulance and the police. They coordinate their response as they manage the incident. Suddenly the separate individuals have become a group of persons. The decisive point occurs when they realize they need each other, not when they first meet as a group. Lewin (1951) described such group creation as the moment when our "fate" is in the hands of others.

Group members, in varying degrees, are involved in the same task even if they have different task experiences and responsibilities. Even when they are participants in the same situation, one can be sure they experience it differently. Their impressions of each other are colored by emotions, associations, and projections that stem from their own life stories. If the members have worked together for a long time, their shared experiences will have refined, confirmed, or refuted these impressions. Despite the group cohesion that develops, the members still behave in ways that reveal their unique and characteristic ways of being. Group members interpret these interactions variously. For example, a word may have one meaning, emotionally and cognitively, for one member but a different meaning for other members. Nevertheless, we may stubbornly continue to talk to others as if the word meant the same thing to everyone. Differences in meanings and emotional responses constantly create communication difficulties when groups of people want to achieve something together.

Group members may talk among themselves about their general work experience, not just about their specific task. Yet their conversations are multilayered; every group member has a unique image of the group. One could say the group has a sociological, external reality, and a psychological, internal reality.

As a manager, if you view the group as a bunch of independent individuals, there is no need to imagine that the group can function with its own dynamics. As a manager, then you have only one option: namely, to engage with group members on a one-to-one basis only. You must address each member's needs, motivations, and interests in a more individualistic way. If you lose the group perspective, you may be tempted to adopt Machiavellian strategies, aimed at enticing or coercing members to do their jobs. This is management by carrots and whips.

However, if you view the group as people who can take responsibility, can relate to others, and can find meaning in purposeful work, you can connect with the group while you consider its degree of maturity (this idea is discussed under the headline

"Group Development"). Wise managers, however, who see the group as an entity are careful not to lose sight of the individuality of each group member.

The group itself is a whole, an organism, in the same way that a biological cell is. We know when we are in a group and when we are not. In a sense, the group is distinct from the world and yet part of the world. Thus, the group has the same relationship to the world that the cell has to the body. Something intangible holds the group together and yet defines its boundaries just as life has both a boundary and an inner dynamic.

A group may not always hold together. It may lack the necessary internal dynamics or may not achieve its task or reach its goal. Such a group outcome may result when the group's members are unable to cooperate because, for example, they have been manipulated or exploited. When a group fails, it may collapse slowly or very suddenly. Such groups often lack a clear purpose, clear boundaries in time and space, and flexible leadership that can respond to change.

Some people are mystified by the idea that the group is a whole, in and of itself. Many people from Western cultures are so focused on individualism that they tend to view the group as merely the sum of its individuals. As an analogy, think of a string quartet or a pop band. Listening to the quartet's or the band's performance is quite different from, for example, listening to a solo violin or a solo guitar. It is the same with a group. There is an atmosphere, a climate, created by "the music of the group" even when the music is cacophonic. A group, like the string quartet or the pop band, needs time for rehearsal, training, and mutual feedback.

As we emphasize in this chapter, the group is a whole that can support or undermine its purpose, depending on how the group members' relationships develop and how well the group's initiatives, communications, and divisions of labor function. Do the members divide and disrupt, or do the members unite and connect? While we are often unaware of a group's dynamics, they exist in what members say and do in their collective interactions.

What Do Groups Do?

The question of what groups do may seem trivial. Yet it is a question worth asking. The idea that groups mostly spend their time and efforts on something completely different than their original task is not completely unfounded (Wilke, 2014). Group members may have very different values and priorities. The group atmosphere may become quite intense when members express their frustrations, anxieties, and even despair. It is easy for groups to be diverted from their main purpose.

If the group forms when members acknowledge their dependence on each other, as Lewin (1951) described, that is the moment when we realize that group emotions are now in play. With the recognition of our mutual dependence, basic human needs assume greater relevancy. Many examples of group dependence are found in the literature on group psychology. We even recognize such dependence in newspaper stories and social media postings that describe peer pressure incidents (e.g., crimes by gang members or strange phenomena observed by sect members).

However, even ordinary work groups seem to lose their ability to think clearly when, for example, a proposed change is perceived as a threat. In such situations, the group's negative and destructive potential is often activated. The group members may blame outsiders for the threat or scapegoat some unfortunate group member. In this way, the group maintains the illusion of group unity and community.

Work Group or Basic Assumption?

The psychoanalyst, Wilfred Bion (1897–1979), in his book on group psychology, described how work groups move between two mental states (Bion, 1969). In the first state, *work*, the group members focus on the task and their roles. The work goes well. Suddenly something disruptive happens. Perhaps an organizational decision to change certain work routines is announced. As described in Chap. 4, the human threat system is extremely sensitive. Due to easily provoked anxieties, the well-functioning work group begins to behave "irrationally" – immediately or gradually. Now the group moves to the second state as the members adopt a *basic assumption*: an "as if" state where the group unconsciously redefines its main task as coping with those anxieties. Less and less work is accomplished. Bion described these "as if" states – the basic assumptions – in terms of "fight-flight," "dependency," and "pairing."

The assumption in fight-flight is that there is a danger that one must flee from or fight against. The assumption in dependency is that the group needs protection from a powerful authority figure who has total responsibility. The group members tend to passively wait for instructions before acting. The assumption in pairing is that two members will form a creative couple, which will generate inspiring ideas, thereby saving the group from doing the work themselves and freeing them from responsibility. For instance, a pair composed of two newcomers to a team facing challenging tasks. Initially the group is charmed by the pair, who get on well with each other, seeing them as an excellent example of youthful brilliance and greeting with enthusiasm the many ideas that they come up with. It takes a week or two for the team to realize that the young couple lacked the experience necessary for a deep understanding of the problem.

The English/American sociologist and group analyst, Earl Hopper, added a fourth basic assumption – "annihilation." This is the assumption that the group will react to traumatic threats either with loss of individual identity, wishing to merge with each other ("massification") or with contact-shunning isolation ("aggregation"). The key expression here is "traumatic threat," i.e., a fear that something bad will happen that threatens the feelings of safety. This could be losing one's job, the introduction of new routines seen as insecure, or a change in the management from a benevolent to an autocratic leadership style. Such events can result in an almost sect-like clinging of the members to each other ("massification"), with a feeling that by doing so they will counteract the threat. The opposite reaction ("aggregation") implies that people avoid each other. They do not speak about what is happening and retreat into isolation, sometimes with clench fists in their pockets. Neither of these dynamics will help the group to cope efficiently with the traumatic threat.

Professionals have observed Bion's and Hopper's group states repeatedly in organizational and clinical settings (Hopper & Weinberg, 2011).

One common problem with such states is that the group members do not realize they have ceased working. On the contrary, they think they are acting responsibly. Managers sometimes despair in such situations. They assume proposed changes will elicit positive responses from everyone. Despite their disappointment in the members' resistance, managers may stubbornly insist on implementing the changes. The risk, then, is that in their frustration and anger, they may lose their ability to think clearly. They also become victims of the basic assumptions.

On the one hand, the group is obviously reacting irrationally when members cease working because they are under the influence of the basic assumptions. However, Bion argues that such behavior is human, understandable, and rational from another viewpoint. He saw the basic assumptions as a way of defending oneself against threatening emotions that group members need time to work through. They might need time to grieve over something that is lost or time to accept the new (and often painful) reality (Bion, 1969). The group's basic assumptions are like the defense mechanisms people use as individuals. For example, in coping with a sudden change, people often act before they consider what a change means. They may react with anger, defensiveness, or frustration. They do not take the time needed to emotionally absorb the effect of the change.

The following example illustrates a basic assumption that a work group at a hospital in a medium-sized Swedish city adopted.

> The work group (i.e., the staff) had just learned that the hospital's only inpatient ward would soon close. Half the staff would lose their jobs. Patients and their relatives would now have to travel long distances for care. The manager called the staff to a crisis meeting to discuss the change. A few minutes before the meeting was to begin, the staff and the manager arrived. They chatted for some time about non-work-related matters such as the many feral cats in the nearby park. Time passed, and the meeting had still not begun. Everyone continued to talk about the cats and other matters. Someone suddenly started talking about his own cat that had kittens recently. Someone else continued the same theme. Fifteen minutes into the meeting, which was the most serious and fatal in the history of the clinic, the entire staff group, including the boss, talked pleasantly about cats.
>
> No one was talking about the momentous change at the hospital. The staff and manager avoided, perhaps unconsciously, any discussion of the stress and anxiety the closure provoked in them. When the manager understood the staff was deliberately avoiding any discussion of this very threatening topic, she began to talk about the closure and the staff's concerns. Gently, she brought everyone back to reality. She said: "Here we are, talking about everyday matters, as we have done together so many times before. We are painfully aware that soon we will not be able to do that anymore. But now it is our job to talk about the closure, and how we will manage that change as well as possible."

In this example, the group used "happy talk" to avoid the topic that was at the back of everyone's mind. The staff used "flight," which is one side of the coin in Bion's fight-flight basic assumption. A different group, to shield itself from the stress and anxiety caused by such a threatening event, might have used another of the basic assumptions. When a group uses the "fight" side of the coin, the group members will behave as if they had someone or something to fight against – not seldom their own manager. In such cases, groups may use banter or cynical remarks to avoid reflection and self-examination. They may try to distance themselves from their true emotions.

When a work group uses a basic assumption, the manager's responsibility is to return the group to its common task in an empathetic way. In unfavorable conditions, however, groups may find themselves more or less permanently stuck in a basic assumption. Then paranoia may spread throughout the organization, resulting in a vicious circle of discouragement and distrust. It is no easy task to reverse such a development. The manager must then work with the group members to create the necessary recovery conditions. For example, perhaps structural changes, updated training, or crisis management programs are needed. Whatever the immediate steps taken, security and predictability in the group must be restored. Nonthreatening conversations and open communications can help revive the precrisis group ambience (Owen, 2008; Wilke, 2014).

Groupthink

Another classic group phenomenon is groupthink. The American social psychologist, Irving Janis (1918–1990), researched group harmony and conformity extensively. He found that groups characterized by destructive groupthink tend to avoid conflict and to support cohesion, even if that means sacrificing critical analysis and tests of their decisions (Janis, 1982). These groups discourage, if not suppress, dissent. Any member who offers a dissenting opinion risks ridicule or mockery. Thus, groupthink all too often results in hasty and irrational decisions caused by the group's reluctance to disrupt the group's balance and shared sense of being on track.

Groupthink is often found among groups in which the members have similar backgrounds, follow authoritarian leaders, and dismiss information from external sources. Historically, many short-term (and disastrous) political decisions have been explained by groupthink. People prone to groupthink often feel invincible and morally superior. They are so convinced of the group's rightness that they may ignore warning signals of possible negative outcomes. They may ridicule and caricature anyone who disagrees with the group's decisions. The consequences can be disastrous.

Groupthink seems to be even more common than Janis (1982) assumed. It may also occur in less catastrophic scenarios and in milder forms. Groupthink builds on strong social identifications with groups, on quests for universal norms, and on the often-unconscious lack of genuine confidence in one's own abilities. Simple solutions to very complex problems are appealing to some people. Groupthink, as explained here, is reminiscent of Erich Fromm's observation on society in his book, *The Escape from Freedom* (1943/1990): Man has traded his autonomy for protection against loneliness.

It requires considerable courage to break the emotional and intellectual paralysis in a groupthink situation by challenging others' poor grasp or lack of facts, illogical reasoning, and general herd mentality. The group's possible recriminations against dissenters are not pleasant to think about.

Psychological Safety

Early in her career, the American leadership researcher and professor at the Harvard Business school Amy Edmondson got unexpected results from an empirical study. She studied group and organizational factors that affected errors in administering drugs to hospitalized patients. She expected to find higher error rates in groups that scored low in perceived unit performance, quality of unit relationships, and nurse manager leadership compared to units that seemed to function well in terms of performance, relationships, and leadership. She found the opposite. In well-functioning work groups, more errors were detected. This finding was certainly counter intuitive and seemed to contradict previous research. However, the findings could be explained, at least partially in this study, by another hypothesis, namely, that well-functioning teams have a shared belief that making a mistake will not be held against anybody. If one can feel safe in that sense it will most likely influence the willingness to report errors, compared to, for example, authoritarian-led groups where nurses might fear the consequences of making a mistake (Edmondson, 1996).

She has later defined *psychological safety* as a shared belief that the team is safe for interpersonal risk taking. This construct was further explored in a manufacturing company, where she found that learning behavior mediated between team psychological safety and team performance. The hypothesis that psychological safety is crucial for organizational learning and performance has been studied repeatedly since then and has solid scientific support (Edmondson, 2018).

In this context, we believe it is important to be aware that psychological safety is a group construct and characterize the group rather than individual members, i.e., the group members must have similar perceptions of it. To understand psychological safety as a group phenomenon implies that learning is an ongoing process of reflection and action between group members. Questions are asked, feedback is sought for, errors or unexpected outcomes of actions are discussed, etcetera (Edmondson, 1999).

The measure of psychological safety originally introduced by Edmondson (1999) has come into use both in research and applied organizational work. It consists of the following items:

1. If you make a mistake on this team, it is often held against you (reversed).
2. Members of this team are able to bring up problems and tough issues.
3. People on this team sometimes reject others for being different (reversed).
4. It is safe to take a risk on this team.
5. It is difficult to ask other members of this team for help (reversed).
6. No one on this team would deliberately act in a way that undermines my efforts.
7. Working with members of this team, my unique skills and talents are valued and utilized.

This scale is used frequently by organizational and leadership consultants and in research. One can speculate that Edmondson's contributions to the field represents a paradigm shift in leadership research (and hopefully in society despite the strength of the counter forces). It originated with Kurt Lewin's research on authoritarian, laissez-faire, and democratic group cultures (Lewin, 1951; Lewin et al., 1939). It is our experience that the authoritarian approach is losing ground in work life, at the same time as it seems to be gaining ground in political life in some parts of the world.

As mentioned above, groupthink in its milder forms is most likely a common phenomenon in work life. Psychological safety can be regarded as the counter point to groupthink. It is a useful construct, with a simple measure (the items above), in the prevention of groupthink.

Independent of Edmondson's research and within another empirical group research tradition one has come to almost identical conclusions regarding the importance of psychological safety but expressed with somewhat different theoretical constructs (Agazarian et al., 2021; Wheelan, 2005a). We will return to this in the next section of this chapter. It relates to the question how groups can develop a culture of psychological safety.

Edmondson has several practical suggestions, such as creating a space for openness. It must be stressed by managers that failures are valuable teachers, that speaking up is important, and that the purpose is to help us to see what is at stake. She advices managers to invite co-workers to take responsibility, to be humble, and not to be afraid to use the sentence "I do not know." It is about creating a sense of being welcomed as equal members (Edmondson, 2018).

In essence, psychological safety is about minimizing the risk for an activation of the biological threat system. Let us in this context elaborate on the SCARF model (Rock & Cox, 2012) mentioned in Chap. 5, which can help managers to think about how to avoid situations which threaten psychological safety. It can also be useful in the analysis of situations that failed, to make it possible to learn from the experience.

The SCARF model consists of the following five dimensions:

Status. People need to be aware of their place in society and at work relative to others. Anything that causes a negative change in status or even suggests that a negative change is possible is perceived as a threat. A stress response is probable. Examples of threatening social cues are public criticism or avoidance by authority figures. Humiliating experiences such as these damage personal dignity and must be avoided if possible or worked through if not possible.

Certainty. This factor is directly related to psychological safety. When threats are perceived, the survival responses of fight, flight, or freeze are activated. These responses can affect emotions and cognition negatively. People must feel safe if they are to think clearly and express opinions freely (Edmondson, 2012, 2018).

Autonomy. Stress research has long established that lack of control or limited decision latitude at work provokes stress responses in the brain (Theorell & Karasek, 1996). Human beings need to feel in control of their lives. Lack of dignity and respect is perceived as a social threat (Deci et al., 2017).

Relatedness. Individual relationships can certainly give rise to both threat and reward responses. However, we argue that *group belonging* is the main social factor, of which individual relations are a part. People need to belong to a group in the family home, at the office, or in other settings. When the group is well-functioning, the sense of relatedness provokes reward responses in the brain, and the system achieves a kind of homeostasis. In groups that function less well, the sense of isolation provokes threat responses that increase the level of stress hormonal activity.

Fairness. Fairness contributes to group cohesion and trust. Group altruism and group cooperation combined with fairness have contributed to group survival during evolution. When we feel unjustly treated, the threat system in the brain is activated; when we feel justly treated, the reward systems in the brain are activated (Stallen et al., 2018). Jaques (1996) argued that equitable payment is one of the most influential factors on co-worker physical and mental health.

The SCARF model provides a general cognitive map of the most important factors in a psychologically safe organizational group culture. In the next section, we will take a closer look on how group processes can support the development of such a culture.

Group Development Theories

At Kurt Lewin's initiative, various group dynamic conferences were held in the United States after World War II. The primary goal of these conferences was to combat racial and religious prejudice. They inspired similar conferences in other countries – for example, at the Tavistock Institute of Human Relations (in England) and at the A. K. Rice Institute for the Study of Social Systems (in the United States). These conferences focused on real-time group processes and their members' experiences of them. Leadership, power, and authority were the main conference topics. In describing the conferences, Bennis and Shepard's (1956) observations significantly influenced subsequent conceptions of group development. One of their observations was that the group seems to develop according to a predetermined pattern.

Group relationship conferences are intended to inform managers, psychologists, researchers, and others about organizational and group psychology through experience-based learning. Bion's theories (1969) are still relevant at these conferences. Systems-centered therapy (SCT), based in part on Bion's theories, has developed into a sophisticated theory of group development (Agazarian, 1998; Gantt & Agazarian, 2005). Others have tried to simplify the Bennis and Shepard model. For example, Will Schutz (1958) developed a theory on interpersonal relations: Fundamental Interpersonal Relations Orientation (FIRO). Bruce Tuckman (1965) identified five phases of group development: forming, storming, norming, performing, and adjourning. The commonality among these theories is the idea that a group must pass through a conflict phase if it is to develop.

Susan Wheelan (2005a, b) concludes from her research on group development that the early group theories have a great deal of scientific support. Groups do develop similarly in a somewhat orderly sequence. In their initial phase, groups process issues that are related to inclusion dominate. Members ask themselves questions about the group's task and about their place in the group, such as the following: Do I want to join this group? Can I add value to this group? Am I capable and competent enough? Do the other members like me? Do I like them? Will I be allowed to participate? The group members must be ready to put these doubts behind them if they are to move forward with enough cohesion and trust that they can focus on their task. It is essential to leave the inclusion stage as soon as possible, because groups are least productive in this early development stage.

Wheelan (2005b) described the following five stages of group's development that she presents in her Integrated Model of Group Development (IMGD) (paraphrased here):

1. *Dependency and inclusion* – Group members depend on a leader to make decisions and issue instructions. Without such leadership, the group cannot work productively. Members are concerned with issues of safety related to inclusion. Because they fear exclusion, they take no unnecessary risks. They accept the group's cultural norms.
2. *Counter-dependency and fight* – Group members discover their dependency on the leader is inhibiting. They want to free themselves from the leader and exert their independence. With an increased sense of safety, members are willing to offer ideas that express their own values and promote different work guidelines. Many opportunities for conflict arise among members. These conflicts must be resolved before the group can move to the next stage.
3. *Trust and structure* – Having resolved their conflicts, group members develop a sense of group cohesion. With trust in each other, group members can now focus on their work. Their communications are more transparent, and their work is more organized and task oriented. It may be difficult to reach this stage in organizations where intense competition is rewarded.
4. *Work and productivity* – Group members understand the group roles, tasks, and goals. They trust each other. Their work becomes more enjoyable and creative. Tasks are viewed as the group responsibility rather than the individual responsibility. Conflicts offer opportunities for further development. The few groups who reach this stage become high-performance teams.
5. *Termination* – Not all groups have a clear ending, but when they have, it must be acknowledged and worked through. Then, it is time to review the work completed and to take farewell on a personal level.

This description of group development in these five stages may suggest the stages are clearly defined and separate. This is not the reality. In fact, groups move back and forth between the stages. Some stages overlap. With subgroups (within the larger group), this irregular stage evolution may be even more complex. One subgroup may be in one stage, while another subgroup is in a different stage.

A crucial point in group development arises when a group crosses the line between stage 2 and stage 3. At this point, the group leaves conflict behind and acquires trust. Wheelan (2005a, b) observed an increase in work productivity and quality when she compared work groups on either side of this line. One explanation is that the group members, having crossed the line, now assume their professional roles. They have learned to focus on work aimed at achieving a common goal (Wheelan & Jacobsson, 2014).

Some critics of Wheelan's IMGD say it is too simple. Other critics argue that groups in the early maturity stages are more capable of performing certain tasks than groups in the later maturity stages. Most theorists on group development, however, agree that groups must pass the conflict stage before group trust can evolve.

Endre Sjøvold, a Norwegian social psychologist, describes how individuals often take different views of the group's work (Sjøvold, 2006). For example, some group members may narrowly focus on the group's task, control, and discipline. Others may focus more broadly on various aspects of the group's work related to relationships, community, care, and trust. When groups polarize vis à vis the group's work in this way, conflict is inevitable. In some instances, depending on the severity of the conflict, the nature of the group task, and the current development stage, it may be necessary to divide the group.

Sjøvold (2006) also addresses the issue of loyalty versus opposition in groups. He concludes that when group members are always "loyal," group development is blocked. He concludes that criticism, opposition, and conflict are needed for group development and even for group survival. In a mature group, members can hold different views and discuss opposing positions calmly. A group is, in fact, more innovative if its members are willing to reconsider their views and positions as conditions and situations change. Much too often, however, less mature group members stubbornly cling to long-held views or positions (cf. "groupthink" above). According to Sjøvold, such members jeopardize group work and productivity.

Management in the Group Development Stages

We examine the manager's leadership role more closely in Chap. 7. In this chapter, we look at the manager's role from the perspective of group development. For the sake of simplicity, we reference Wheelan's five stages. According to Wheelan (2005a, b), managers must adapt their leadership style as groups move through the five development stages.

In the first stage – *the dependency and inclusion stage* – managers must take control as they introduce the work group members to each other and to the whole group. The managers should emphasize the organizational goals, provide information, and check and clarify routines. They should help the members understand the nature and purpose of the work. This means explaining members' roles while supporting them with positive feedback.

A work group's goals may change when the conditions surrounding the organization change. Furthermore, group members often have different opinions and interpretations of the goals, leading to conflicts. To develop, the group needs sufficient opportunity to discuss these opinions and interpretations and sufficient time to resolve these conflicts. Wheelan (2005a) argued that the importance of group goals changes during the group's evolution. These initial discussions about goals act as icebreakers as members become acquainted with each other. The group's real work is delayed until later stages.

If, as a manager, you support co-worker participation, individual responsibility, and personal development, you may feel uncomfortable assuming authority in the group. You might object a bit to such "old-fashioned" leadership. However, while the group is in the dependency and inclusion stage, it needs a reliable authority to lean on. We caution that this leadership style should be exercised wisely so that it does not slide into destructive authoritarianism.

Research has shown that groups develop faster if they begin with a clear structure where the group's goals can be presented (Wheelan, 2005b). Unfortunately, some self-important managers are disinclined to relax control when the group is ready to move to the next stage. These managers pose an obstacle to the group's development. They are unlikely to understand the source of the group members' negative responses in the next stage.

In the second stage – *the counter-dependency and fight stage* – managers must avoid responding to such negativity too personally. We do not underestimate the rejection, even anger, that managers feel when group members challenge them. It is always difficult to convince yourself that challenges to your authority are not personal attacks. Managers, even under such stress, should maintain the focus on conflict resolution and reduction of tension. At these times, group members need managers' assistance. Regrettably, some managers (or influential group members), who find conflict too disturbing, reverse group progress by returning to the dependency scenario of the first stage.

In the third stage – *the trust and structure stage* – managers benefit from the cohesion and trust in the group that is the outcome of their work on conflict resolution and tension reduction in the second stage. Managers can now step back somewhat from their role as authority figures. They can delegate some leadership tasks to capable group members. Managers in this stage earn the respect of the group members by demonstrating their managerial competence, focus, and empathy (among other qualities). In this way, managers encourage member participation.

In the fourth stage – *the work and productivity stage* – managers have confidence that the group members understand the group's goals and ways of working. The managerial role is now more about work vision, expertise, and resources. Group members look to the managers for their expertise. Many leadership responsibilities can now be assumed by the members most qualified to lead.

While some managers are reluctant to withdraw from the active leadership role, others feel almost liberated when they can delegate responsibility to the group. They are ready to take a different role, perhaps as experts, in the work of a well-functioning group. In fact, it is extremely stimulating to work in a well-functioning and productive group. It's an experience we wish that more people could have.

Unfortunately, it seems that only 50% of work groups reach stages 3 and 4, at least as indicated by a study of work groups in the United States and Sweden (Wheelan & Jacobsson, 2014).

In our practice as psychologists and consultants, we have counseled cynical, exhausted, self-blaming, or unmotivated managers who exhibit signs of stress and poor health when their groups do not develop beyond the counter-dependency and fight stage. The tragedy is that more work groups could reach the fourth stage if the necessary conditions in terms of a supportive organizational environment and insightful leadership were present.

Work group members and managers in the fourth stage enjoy considerable job satisfaction. They are comfortable with the more relaxed control structure. The paradox is that the group members in this stage often do not rate their managers highly in leadership surveys. These members do not see their managers as leaders in the same way as leadership is traditionally understood and operationalized in such surveys. Managers in the dependency stage may score higher. It seems a fairer survey of managerial leadership should place greater value on group functioning, including psychological safety, than on day-to-day leadership. Three researchers have developed alternative ways to evaluate leadership in response to this shortcoming in traditional leadership surveys: the Group Development Questionnaire, GDQ (Wheelan, 2005a); the Systematized Person-Group Relations, SPGR (Sjøvold, 2007); and Psychological Safety (Edmondson, 1999).

Co-workers' Roles and Responsibilities

The literature on leadership viewed from the perspective of the leader is extensive. However, much less literature on leadership viewed from the perspective of the co-worker is available. However, as researchers in recent years have focused more on the interdependence between managers and co-workers, co-workership has become a topic of greater research interest. The complexity of globalization with its fierce competition, superfast network communications, and the pressure to increase efficiency has also spurred interest in the co-worker role (Sundlin & Sundlin, 2014). One result of these changes in the business world is that co-workers must act more independently in their networks and groups, often outside the knowledge and control of their managers. In addition, as the size of work groups has increased, more forms of joint or shared leadership have emerged (Denis et al., 2012; Döös et al., 2017).

Co-workers who move between groups bring with them useful knowledge of how groups function and evolve. Their previous experience with group productivity and creativity is an especially valuable intangible asset that can be used to promote cohesion among managers and co-workers in other groups. Moreover, the experience they have acquired as leaders of subgroups has made them more professional. It is an important task of managers to contribute to co-workers' development in their roles. This will make them welcomed as members of the different groups they join and facilitate for them to take their different roles with authority.

References

Agazarian, Y. M. (1998). *Systems-centered therapy for groups*. Karnac.

Agazarian, Y. M., Gantt, S. P., & Carter, F. B. (2021). *Systems-centered training*. Routledge.

Alvinius, A., Wilde Larsson, B., & Larsson, G. (2016). Managing boundaries in integrated care – A qualitative study of collaboration between municipalities and county councils in Sweden. *International Journal of Organization Theory and Behavior, 19*(2), 139–165.

Bennis, W. G., & Shepard, H. A. (1956). A theory of group development. *Human Relations, 9*, 415–437.

Bion, W. R. (1969). *Experiences in groups and other papers*. Routledge. ISBN 9780415040204.

Deci, E. L., Olafsen, A. H., & Ryan, R. M. (2017). Self-determination theory in work organizations: The state of a science. *Annual Review of Organizational Psychology and Organizational Behavior, 4*, 19–43.

Denis, J.-L., Langley, A., & Sergi, V. (2012). Leadership in the plural. *The Academy of Management Annals, 6*(1), 211–283.

Döös, M., Vinell, H., & von Knorring, M. (2017). Going beyond "two-getherness": Nurse managers' experiences of working together in a leadership model where more than two share the same chair. *Intensive & Critical Care Nursing, 43*, 39–46.

Edmondson, A. C. (1996). Learning from mistakes is easier said than done: Group and organizational influences on the detection and correction of human error. *The Journal of Applied Behavioral Science, 32*(1), 5–28.

Edmondson, A. C. (1999). Psychological safety and learning behavior in work teams. *Administrative Science Quarterly, 44*(2), 350–383.

Edmondson, A. C. (2012). *Teaming. How organizations learn, innovate, and compete in the knowledge economy*. Jossey-Bass.

Edmondson, A. C. (2018). *The fearless organization. Creating psychological safety in the workplace for learning, innovation and growth*. Wiley.

Fromm, E. (1943/1994). *Escape from freedom*. Henry Holt Company Inc.

Gantt, S. P., & Agazarian, Y. M. (2005). *SCT in action. Applying the systems-centered approach in organizations*. iUniverse Inc.

Hackman, J. R. (2002). *Leading teams. Setting the stage for great performances*. Harvard Business School Press.

Hopper, E., & Weinberg, H. (2011). *The social unconscious in persons, groups and societies mainly theory*. Routledge.

Jacobsson, C., Rydbo, N., & Börresen, J.-E. (2014). The links between group development and health in manufacturing industry. *Small Group Research, 45*, 400–415.

Janis, I. L. (1982). *Groupthink*. Houghton Mifflin.

Jaques, E. (1996). *Requisite Organization. A total system for effective managerial organization and managerial leadership for the 21st century*. Arlington, VA, Cason Hall.

Kozlowski, S. W. J., & Ilgen, D. R. (2006). Enhancing the effectiveness of work groups and teams. *Psychological Science in the Public Interest, 7*(3), 77–124.

Levine, J. M., & Moreland, R. L. (1990). Progress in small group research. *Annual Review of Psychology, 41*, 585–634.

Lewin, K. (1951). *Field theory in social science*. Harper & Row.

Lewin, K., Lippit, R., & White, R. K. (1939). Patterns of aggressive behavior in experimentally created social climates. *Journal of Social Psychiatry, 10*, 271–301.

Lieberman, M. D. (2014). *Social: Why our brains are wired to connect*. Crown Publishing Group.

Lyubovnikova, J., West, M. A., Dawson, J. F., & Carter, M. R. (2015). 24-Karat or fool's gold? Consequences of real team and co-acting group membership in healthcare organizations. *European Journal of Work and Organizational Psychology, 24*(6), 929–950.

Owen, H. (2008). *Open space technology: A user's guide*. Berrett-Koehler.

Rock, D., & Cox, C. (2012). SCARF in 2012: Updating the social neuroscience of collaborating with others. *Neuro Leadership Journal, 4*(4), 1–16.

Rozovsky, U. (2015). *The five keys to a successful Google team*. https://rework.withgoogle.com/blog/five-keys-to-a-successful-google-team/

Salas, E., Tannenbaum, S. I., Cohen, D. J., & Latham, G. (Eds.). (2013). *Developing and enhancing teamwork in organizations. Evidence-based best practice and guidelines*. Jossey-Bass.

Sandahl, C., Nilsson Ahlin, H., Asklin-Westerdahl, C., Björling, M., Malmquist Saracino, A., Wennlund, L., Åkerström, U., & Örhammar, A. (2021). *Why group therapy works and how to do it. A guide for health and social care professionals*. Routledge.

Schutz, W. C. (1958). *FIRO: A three-dimensional theory of interpersonal behavior*. Rinehart.

Sjövold, E. (2006). Maturity and effectiveness in small groups. *Nordic Psychology, 58*(1), 43–56.

Sjövold, E. (2007). Systematizing Person-Group Relations (SPGR): A field theory of social interaction. *Small Group Research, 38*(5), 615–635. https://doi.org/10.1177/1046496407304334

Söderhjelm, T. (2018). *Teaming over time: Team and team leadership development through different interventions*. Dissertation, Karolinska Institutet.

Stallen, M., Rossi, F., Heijne, A., Smidts, A., De Dreu, C., & Sanfey, A. G. (2018). Neurobiological mechanisms of responding to injustice. *The Journal of Neuroscience, 38*(12), 2944–2954. https://doi.org/10.1523/JNEUROSCI.1242-17.2018

Sundlin, A.-L., & Sundlin, P. (2014). *Taking up your role: How to shift between life and work without losing yourself.* Catalyst Communications Press.

Sundlin, A. L., Söderhjelm, T. M., & Sandahl, C. (2022). Making rapid shifts in work roles – An essential teamwork skill. An exploratory study of facilitating and inhibiting factors. *Team Performance Management: An International Journal* (ahead-of-print).

Theorell, T., & Karasek, R. A. (1996). Current issues relating to psychosocial job strain and cardiovascular disease research. *Journal of Occupational Health Psychology, 1*(1), 9–26. https://doi.org/10.1037/1076-8998.1.1.9. (Retraction published 1995, Stress Medicine, 11[1], 17-26).

Tuckman, B. W. (1965). Developmental sequences in small groups. *Psychological Bulletin, 63*, 384–399.

Wheelan, S. A. (2005a). *Creating effective teams: A guide for members and leaders*. Sage.

Wheelan, S. A. (2005b). *Group processes. A developmental perspective*. Allyn and Bacon.

Wheelan, S. (2009). Group size, group development, and group productivity. *Small Group Research, 40*(2), 247–262.

Wheelan, S. A., & Jacobsson, C. (2014). A descriptive study of work groups in the Swedish and US economy. In *The 9th GRASP conference*. Linköping University.

Wilke, G. (2014). *The art of group analysis in organisations. The use of intuitive and experiential knowledge*. Karnac.

Woods, S., & West, M. A. (2019). *The psychology of work and organisations* (3rd ed.). Cengage Publishing.

Leading as a Manager

7

The manager is a catalyst of the collective potential of the co-workers.

In daily work life, managing means creating conditions and supervising situations competently so that co-workers can work in a coordinated and purposeful way. Building trust is a cornerstone in managerial leadership; it is an asset that cannot be measured in the traditional way, but eventually it will turn up in the balance sheet.

Most people think they know a good leader when they see one. Many people name Nelson Mandela and Mahatma Gandhi when asked to identify leadership role models. As we discussed in Chap. 2, great leaders evoke the great man theory of leadership from the nineteenth century. This theory proposes that leaders (typically men) are heroes who change the world by their natural skills and special personality traits (Wahl, 2014). Other people, who have a more complex theory of great leadership, think situational factors influence the rise of great leaders. An example could be the Ukrainian president, Volodymyr Zelensky, who proved himself a national leader when the Russian army invaded his country in 2022. However, most of us have observed that leadership skills and traits can be acquired in less dramatic circumstances, such as when someone unexpectedly emerges as a leader in the workplace, in sports, or in other contexts.

Regardless of whether their leadership skills and traits were inborn or acquired, few leaders can match the role models exemplified by Mandela or Gandhi – or are expected to. Normally, we do not look for world-changing leadership models, for example, among CEOs of publicly held companies, heads of international foundations, or even national presidents and prime ministers. We may expect greater personal maturity from persons in such highly influential positions. We may look for the leaders who exercise authority in the way Marcus Aurelius (the Roman emperor and Stoic philosopher) did rather than leaders who exercise the kind of brute power described by Machiavelli (the sixteenth-century diplomat and author).

C. Sandahl, M. von Knorring, *Managing with Sense and Sensitivity*,
https://doi.org/10.1007/978-3-031-24109-3_7

However, we certainly do not expect, for example, top managers in industry, first-line managers in elder care, research supervisors at pharmaceutical companies, or school principals to change history.

When we explore leadership further, we often find role models near us who are quite relatable. Perhaps a grandfather, a teacher, an older sibling, a parent, or a religious mentor is your role model. Considerable variability in leadership role models is even found in work groups. Some group leaders are regarded as role models based on their empathy and support; others, based on their reliability and decisiveness. Members of the same work group may not agree on who is a good leader and who is not.

As a manager, it is likely you will find such diverse leadership opinions in your work group. Some group members will view your leadership positively, others negatively. After a few years, most managers, to a certain extent, have to accept negative evaluations of their leadership as a painful reality. However, acceptance does not mean you should cynically conclude you will not try to be more approachable, more supportive, more decisive, or whatever else your co-workers think you should be. If you adopt an "I don't care" leadership attitude, the situation will not change and may even become worse.

Before looking closely at the everyday work of managers, we should think about the work conditions that influence a manager's success or failure. The organization's governance systems are the most influential of these conditions. We need to know how these systems were established and implemented, how they have been interpreted and used, and how they interact with each other. Governance systems at most organizations are a mix of bureaucratic controls (e.g., rules, laws, and regulations), management systems (e.g., policies and plans), and collegial controls (e.g., the use of professionals' knowledge and expertise).

Governance systems can create as well as solve problems. For example, detailed bureaucratic control systems for documenting procedures and following-up on outcomes can divert a disproportionate amount of time and energy from essential work tasks. Or data, collected at significant cost, may not be used. Management control systems aimed at greater work efficiency can be unreasonably harsh and demotivating. Collegial control systems, in the worst case, can lead to rivalries among professionals or work groups that damage co-worker cooperation and organizational productivity.

Managers can contribute to the design of governance systems in ways that support organizations' visions and help achieve their goals. The more managers know about the strengths and weaknesses of such systems, the better equipped they are to help with their design. Governance systems influence, among other things, the extent to which a manager "must" sit in meetings and drive change initiatives that lack foundation and purpose for the organization. To avoid such situations, managers should promote the use of systems that facilitate their cooperation with other managers and, most important, facilitate their communications with top management. In addition, managers should demand control systems that specify their responsibilities, that identify available resources, and that set performance evaluation criteria. Without the support of their superiors, managers may flounder directionless as they gradually lose the trust of their co-workers and of top management.

Managers' Everyday Work

When people read management and organization literature or scan advertisements for managerial positions, they may wonder at the elevated language used to describe leaders. Leadership today is often about "big issues"– visions, high-minded ideals, and global problems. The implicit (and usually explicit) message is that good leaders are charismatic, decisive, and creative. They have superior strategic and tactical skills. Thus, top executives may conclude that what many people regard as excessive executive compensation is not only justified but also equitable. It may be worrying, if not intimidating, for managers – or would-be managers – who are more accustomed to dealing with smaller problems to read these descriptions. Possibly you can boost your ego with the thought that you, too, are a member of this elite group.

The manager's typical work rarely involves formulating visions, drawing up strategies, or parading around as the charismatic leader (Alvesson, 2017; Alvesson & Sveningsson, 2003). Many middle managers have insufficient time for planning and reflection. They are too busy managing everyday tasks: responding to urgent requests, solving production and personnel problems, and metaphorically putting out fires – all the while, talking and listening to co-workers (Styhre, 2012a, b). In practice, everyday management is about making short-term plans, attending meetings, and (more rarely) making decisions that no one else can make.

Tyrstrup (2006) argued in an empirical study that leaders' strategies in practice emerge spontaneously from activities that have already taken place at different levels in the organization. Tyrstrup's findings confirmed research by Karl Weick (an American organizational theorist), namely, that leaders' strategies are often ex post constructions that explain, reasonably and comprehensibly, why events occurred as they did and why leaders acted as they did. In this theory, leaders improvise and construct their leadership after events so as to understand those events (Holmberg, 2012; Holmberg & Tyrstrup, 2010; Weick, 1995). The important task for the manager in such cases is to contribute to making sense of what has already happened.

Researchers have spent considerable effort trying to pinpoint exactly what makes leadership in daily practice so chaotic, difficult, and stressful (Alvesson & Sveningsson, 2003; Larsson & Lundholm, 2010). *Good to Great: Why Some Companies Make the Leap and Others Don't* (Collins, 2001) was a best-selling book that explored leadership style. For his research, Jim Collins studied some of the most successful, late-twentieth-century American companies and their leaders. He found these leaders were modest and reasonable rather than charismatic and arrogant. All were driven by the wish to act in their company's best interest and to make a positive contribution to society. His research, however, has been criticized on several grounds. Among other things, it is charged that the book features a small and select sample of companies. Leadership at such companies, according to this criticism, is context dependent. Collins's findings may be unreliable when generalized to other social and historical circumstances. Furthermore, it is easy to think of several internationally successful companies whose leaders can hardly be described as modest or unselfish. Nevertheless, Collins's research shows us that we can also identify successful international companies led by people who are unpretentious, humanitarian, and driven by the wish to contribute to society's advancement.

Successful leaders in the corporate world are, of course, interesting to study. However, they may not always be seen as role models by the many mid-level managers who every day, far from the limelight, solve problems, implement policy, uphold standards and values, and manage everything else they are tasked with.

Managers' and Co-workers' Health and Well-being

The job of the manager is demanding, important, interesting, and stimulating. It should meet the classic criterion of "good work," in which jobholders have some measure of job control and can adapt the job requirements to their experience and skills (Karasek & Theorell, 1992). Furthermore, a reasonable balance between effort and reward is expected in good work (Siegrist, 1996). As a manager, to some extent you can create the space needed to make decisions and to exercise control. If you lack this ability, you are unlikely to find your work meaningful. However, if your competence and skills match the position's demands, your superiors are supportive, the position offers professional growth possibilities, and the compensation is fair, the risk of work-related stress associated with the position may be minimal (Jaques, 1996).

The one factor that may create the most stress in the manager's job is the manager-co-worker relationship. Co-workers are a major part of the manager's work environment. When co-workers are dissatisfied, unmotivated, and stressed, the pressure on managers naturally increases. In such situations, as a manager you may take impulsive, emotion-driven actions that have little positive effect. In fact, your actions may well exacerbate the situation. Your own and your co-workers' stress levels will probably increase sharply.

We are unable to identify any research that examines how co-workers affect managers' stress levels. However, research exists that compares managers and non-managers in terms of various stress-inducing factors at work (e.g., co-worker conflicts, work overload and pressure, lack of job control, and job insecurity). The findings indicate that while work-related, stress-inducing demands in general are greater for managers than for non-managers, managers deal with stress better because of their greater workplace decision latitude. If managers have sufficient space and time to reflect on the causes of their stress, they are better able to cope with conflict situations (Bernin & Theorell, 2001; Johansson et al., 2013). Managers especially need this space and time when conflict situations arise in which co-workers pressure managers, for example, by seeing them as the actual cause of work problems (see Chaps. 6 and 8).

Other research has addressed the effect of managers on co-workers' stress levels. A typical example of such research is a study in which work demands and control played a mediating role in the relationship between co-workers' distress and their leaders' behavior (Lornudd et al., 2015). This study suggests that managers can reduce co-workers' stress levels by setting reasonable work demands and relaxing rigid controls. With an increase in their work autonomy and flexibility, co-workers have less work-related stress.

There is some evidence that managers' leadership style influences co-workers' health and general well-being, both positively and negatively (Nyberg et al., 2009). For example, Nyberg and her co-authors reached the startling conclusion that male co-workers' positive opinions of their managers were associated with a decreased risk of morbidity and mortality from cardiovascular disease (corrected for other risk factors such as stress and smoking) – even 10 years after they completed their first questionnaire. According to this study, co-workers who agreed with the following statements had a reduced risk of death from a heart attack, especially if they had worked for the same manager for several consecutive years (p. 640).

1. My boss gives me the information I need.
2. My boss is good at pushing through and carrying out changes.
3. My boss explains goals and subgoals for our work so that I understand what they mean for my particular part of the work.
4. I have a clear picture of what my boss expects of me.
5. My boss shows that he/she cares how things are for me and how I feel.
6. I have sufficient power in relation to my responsibilities.
7. My boss takes the time to become involved in his/her employees' professional development.
8. My boss encourages my participation in the scheduling of my work.
9. I am praised by my boss if I have done something good.
10. I am criticized by my boss if I have done something that is not good.

Nyberg et al.'s (2009) study supports the idea that good leadership, given the above operational definition, has a positive effect on co-workers' health and well-being. This conclusion challenges the hypothesis that "bad is stronger than good" proposed by Skogstad et al. (2014a) in a study on the power of destructive leadership (see Chap. 2). We think that both are correct. Destructive leadership has immediate and dramatic negative consequences, which will last until there is a change of the situation. Good leadership, on the other hand, usually goes unnoticed, and it will take some time for the positive consequences to become apparent.

Destructive leadership can certainly have strong consequences. Managers who act aggressively, impulsively, fraudulently, or unpredictably undermine their own authority in the long run. Co-workers' responses to such managerial behavior are predictable: suspicion, resistance, complaints, and disrespect. However, the actively destructive leader has a curious advantage compared to the passive, laissez-faire, non-visible manager. Co-workers may respond to the actively destructive manager with obvious demonstrations of resentment and hatred. However, the passively destructive manager creates only a vague sense of discomfort, stress, and irritation among co-workers. Then, it is difficult for managers to identify the causes of the co-workers' dissatisfaction. The risk even increases that the co-workers will turn against each other (Fors Brandebo & Alvinius, 2019).

Managers must act courageously when dealing with destructive actions committed by upper management or by co-workers. Passive acceptance of such situations by managers will undermine their authority, damage their trust relationships, and put at risk the accomplishment of agreed-upon organizational goals. Therefore, managers must act independently and reject any pressure or exploitation. This is certainly not an easy task. Before taking action in response to such destructive actions, it might sometimes be wise to consult a trusted senior colleague or a consultant from outside the organization.

The appointment of new managers can sometimes have dramatic effects. Within a few weeks, an ill-functioning manager can destroy the work climate in a satisfied and productive work group who previously did not reflect much about their manager's leadership because there were no disruptions. Disruptions can occur, for example, when a new manager impatiently changes normal routines or exhibits an authoritarian leadership style that differs from previous managers' relaxed leadership styles. As stress-related symptoms appear among co-workers, absenteeism may increase, and productivity may decrease.

Despite efforts to increase our understanding in this area, we still lack some knowledge of the complexities of the manager-co-worker relationship and its effects on the health and well-being of both groups. However, the available evidence suggests there is a linkage. Most research focuses on co-workers' opinions of managers or on co-workers' job satisfaction. Thus, we know a good deal about the manager-co-worker relationship from this perspective. It seems reasonable to infer that co-worker job satisfaction is associated with their health and well-being and that co-workers' opinions of their managers reveal facts about their managers' behavior. For example, Nyberg (2009) found, in line with findings from research on the "dark side of leadership" (Fors Brandebo & Alvinius, 2019), that authoritarian, manipulative, unfair, or self-centered managers negatively influence co-workers' job satisfaction, health, and well-being. Of the destructive forms, avoidant leadership seems to be the strongest predictor of negative stress among employees (Skogstad et al., 2014b).

In summary, the research indicates that co-workers' health and well-being are positively influenced by managers who employ co-workers' skills productively, who are concerned about co-workers' wellness, who respond to signs of co-workers' distress, and who provide constructive support to co-workers. Numerous researchers have made the argument that mentally and physically healthy co-workers will deliver positive results in terms of quality goods and services. Over time, these results account for companies' sustainable survival (Conradie et al., 2016; Fabius et al., 2013, 2016; Grossmeier et al., 2016; Lohela-Karlsson et al., 2015).

Do Managers Form Their Leadership in a Vacuum?

A popular assumption among both managers and their co-workers is that leaders unilaterally take advantage of individual circumstances and create their leadership style independently of situations or relationships. Managers, however, while protecting their autonomy, must also be aware of their dependence on their work context. Given what we know about groups and organizations as systems (see Chaps. 6 and 8), it is a deficient and misleading view of leadership to believe that a leadership style is determined only by one's decisions. Two principal factors determine how leadership is exercised (i.e., how favorable conditions set the stage for meaningful and effective work). These factors are, first, the manager's personality and experience, and, second, the organization's policies, culture, mandates, and resources combined with co-workers' response and support. These factors set limits on what is possible at work. If, for example, top management exhibits a cynical and repressive attitude that discourages a learning culture or an investment in co-workers' development, that attitude will be contagious as it spreads to lower levels. Of course, the reverse is also true. If managers treat co-workers with dignity and respect, co-workers are likely to respond in kind (Larsson et al., 2005).

Co-workers, in various ways, co-create managers' leadership. They play a crucial role in interpreting, communicating, and implementing managers' implicit intentions and explicit directions. It is also important the extent to which co-workers share the organization's goals and take responsibility for achieving them. However, some co-workers may try to influence your leadership in ways you did not intend or direct, because they think they are entitled to undermine or challenge your authority. In both cases, co-workers influence your leadership style. In the first case, you should recognize that good outcomes are also the result of the work group's competence and efforts and the organization's norms and routines. Such outcomes probably have very little to do with your particular contributions. In the second case, you should recognize that, in a typically human reaction, people may be inclined to take revenge on rebellious co-workers. In such situations, it is better to think carefully before taking action. Exactly what to do depends on several factors that include the group dynamics, history, and organizational culture and your own experience. It is essential to control your possible immediate and angry responses, to suppress expressions of disappointment, and to take time for calm reflection. A wise idea is to discuss the situation with a colleague or friend as you plan the appropriate response.

Leadership is certainly not created by managers in a vacuum. Leadership is produced by the manager as a human being (with the strengths and weaknesses of the human condition), by the organization in its environment (with its advantages and disadvantages), and by the co-workers (with their positive and negative relationships with management). Productivity, work quality, and profitability to some extent depend on how managers exercise their leadership. However, it is rare that only one of several factors determines how successful an organization is in achieving its purpose and goals (Woods & West, 2019).

In other words, managers depend on their co-workers and on the organization as represented by top management. Exercising leadership is thus largely about jointly managing relationships and dealing with situations that arise, frequently and predictably, in daily work. This manager-co-worker dependency is mutual. How managers understand the organization's mission and tasks and their way of being also affect the work environment, the organizational culture, and co-workers' health and engagement. Leadership, therefore, requires examination not only of the organization's technical and financial resources, collaboration structures, suppliers, and customers but also – and most importantly – managers' self-awareness.

Co-workers decide how they will react to managers' expectations of them. They also decide how they will respond to the positive or negative feedback they receive from managers. In both instances, co-workers have the power to accept or reject managers' claim to authority. Given top management approval, managers have the power to control co-workers' actions. However, managers' experience of being in control is a consequence of co-workers' reactions (i.e., how well co-workers accept managers' authority). According to some researchers, managers' control does not *cause* co-workers' responses or actions (Grint, 2005; Larsson & Lundholm, 2013). Other researchers (e.g., Jackson & Parry, 2008), who confirm this insight, emphasize that leadership cannot be studied in isolation. Managers are individuals, but their leadership is a function of group dynamics.

Simply stated, it is not always easy to decide who is a leader and who is a follower. Because of this conundrum, managers sometimes feel powerless even when they are not. Quite a lot of thoughtful self-processing by managers is needed before they understand that managerial leadership and co-worker collaboration are parts of the same whole. Because their dependency is mutual, co-workers are the prerequisite for leadership, and leadership is the prerequisite for co-workership. With this understanding in mind, you can realize your potential as a manager without overemphasizing your own importance. Then, you can shape your leadership based on the dynamics of the organization as a whole and in interaction with the group of people you manage. Managers who understand their "way of being" and accept their responsibilities positively influence the work environment that is so critical to the health and well-being of their co-workers – and for the outcome of their joint efforts to achieve the organization's goals and mission.

What Do Managers Really Do?

To summarize the ideas presented in this section, we have further developed a model presented by Sandahl et al. (2004) inspired by previous research (Carlson, 1951; Mintzberg, 1973; Tengblad, 2012). This model, *the Managerial Leadership Grid (MLG)* (see Fig. 7.1) shows what managers do – *what* tasks managers should perform and *how* they should perform those tasks.

Let us start with the *what*, i.e., what managers do. One of the most important managerial functions is to clarify the organization's purpose: what the organization stands for, where it is headed, and how it plans to get there (this will be further developed in Chap. 8). This kind of clarification and dialogue points to the path that co-workers will take as they strive to achieve their goals, given the boundaries of the

LEADERSHIP / MANAGEMENT	**Be a role model** (*Judgement*)	**Show consideration** (*Social competence*)	**Contribute to meaning and coherence** (*Motivation*)
Managing day-to-day operations	Make decisions Solve daily problems	Represent Communicate clearly	Provide clear goals and structure
Supervising co-workers	Make demands and give fair rewards Organize for employee participation	Give support and confront	Coach and delegate responsibility
Managing change	Show civil courage Long term planning	Contain insecurity and projections	Inspire to see purpose and meaning with work
Delegating	Monitor allocation of resources	Be an efficient group member	Contribute with expert knowledge and visionary thinking

Fig. 7.1 The managerial leadership grid, MLG

work group within the system. This process is not about giving direction. It is about listening and discovering the contributions of the co-workers. The role of the manager is to be a catalyst for the organization's work.

Most managers understand that their work consists of various tasks, some of which are major, others minor. These tasks include ensuring the workplace is functional, hiring the right staff, and issuing instructions and other communications. Regardless of the size and complexity of the tasks, managers find that human relations and thereby also emotions are involved.

One way of describing what managers really do is to examine the following four primary managerial tasks. Each task presents emotional challenges for the manager, which belongs to the relational aspect of the different tasks. In MLG, *the categories define the practice of management*. The categories are certainly different in terms of content, between managers in different types of organizations, and different levels in the hierarchy. However, first-line managers, middle managers, and CEOs all have to deal with the following types of tasks (Fig. 7.1, the rows in the grid):

- Managing day-to-day operations.
- Supervising co-workers.
- Managing change.
- Delegating.

Another way of categorizing is to look at the relational and emotional aspects of managerial leadership. In Chap. 3, we described transformational leadership in terms of a proactive, inclusive, encouraging, and supportive approach in relationships with co-workers. Here, we use the categories developed at the Swedish National Defense College. The categories are an adaptation of the theory of transformational and authentic leadership (Larsson et al., 2018). There is some support from research that such leadership have a positive effect on the group by increasing its efficiency, well-being, and profitability (Avolio & Gardner, 2005).

Regardless of the adjective used to describe leadership style, researchers and commentators generally use a mix of the same words to describe the most important leadership qualities: trust, predictability, integrity, empathy, resilience, and humility – to name only six of these qualities. In the Larsson et al. (2018) approach, leadership is presented as three requirements (Fig. 7.1, the columns in the grid):

1. Be a role model.
2. Show consideration.
3. Contribute to meaning and coherence.

In our understanding, these requirements relate to three broader metapsychological categories: (1) judgment, (2) social competence, and (3) motivation. In MLG, *these categories define the basic requirements for exercising leadership.*

We created MLG to examine management and leadership in terms of what managers do. The model presents four types of management tasks (the furthermost left vertical column) and the three recommended leadership dimensions (the top horizontal column). However, the main point of the grid are not the categories but the different types of managerial leadership actions exemplified in the boxes of the grid. Think of it as equivalent to the periodic table of chemical elements. The rows and the columns represent certain characteristic of each element. Here, we tentatively suggest 12 managerial leadership elements in terms of typical actions taken by managers. Looking at it from this perspective, it becomes obvious *that leadership and management in terms of practice cannot be separated; they are two sides of the same coin.* It is about *what* to do (management) and *how* to do it (leadership).

Let us exemplify with one of the tasks described in the first box: *to make decisions.* As a manager, one can take decisions on one's own based on rapid thought processes or intuition. It can work if everything is identical to the last time the same problem was encountered, but most of the time this is not the case. To avoid the problem to return soon again in a new shape, one has to use one's judgment to analyze the situation, contemplate alternatives, and consider short- and long-term consequences, including the effects for oneself. Is it possible to live with the consequences? As a manager, I must ask myself if I can "walk the talk," i.e., to be a role model.

Users of the model will differ as to which of the 12 leadership elements they emphasize and which they find challenging. Users will also emphasize different elements at different times when they have a managerial role.

No one can excel in all the model's leadership elements. When we have shown the model to managers, most of them say they are confident they are good at two or three elements. They also differ in their interpretation of "good" in this context. They agree that the model envisions an ideal, probably an unattainable ideal. Nevertheless, they find the model useful as a tool for identifying their strengths and weaknesses in various situations. For example, if managers are aware of their hesitancy and self-doubt in a situation, they can better manage that situation. Perhaps they will take time to analyze the cause of their concerns, or they may discuss the situation with a colleague. When managers learn which elements of their leadership are less "good," they can solicit relevant feedback from co-workers and top management.

Next, we will discuss the four managerial tasks in more detail (Fig. 7.1, the rows of the grid).

Managing Day-to-Day Operations

As a manager, you are responsible for the organization's day-to-day operations, including meetings and contacts with operational and support staff, suppliers, customers, advisors, and other stakeholders, both inside and outside the organization. You also make numerous decisions (urgent and otherwise). You help build a structure designed to facilitate the achievement of the organization's goals and to create trust in the organization by using standardized routines and workflows. Although research shows that organizational structures can contribute to organizational trust, structures that are too rigid can contribute to organizational distrust. Co-workers, for example, who place a high value on their independence may become angry and frustrated if their freedom of action at work is too tightly restricted or if they are not allowed to express their opinions (Edmondson, 2018).

Tyrstrup (2006) observed that almost half a manager's time is spent dealing with unanticipated events that require immediate decisions. According to Tyrstrup, managers who are faced with such situations must be ready to act even if all the facts are not yet known. They need the ability to improvise on the spot. Badaracco (2002) is of the opinion that such improvisation is dependent on timing to be successful. When in doubt, it might be advisable to wait and see. He argues that leadership often needs to be exercised quietly, sometimes by restraining the impulse to take immediate action in crisis situations. Managers must involve themselves fully by taking both an emotional perspective and an intellectual perspective in difficult situations – even if the struggle between the two perspectives means sleepless nights. Such involvement requires that managers have this good sense of timing. Often one needs to "buy some time" so that one can find compromises without breaking the rules, even if one might occasionally need to bend them somewhat. Sometimes the problem is resolved without any intervention from the manager. Quiet leaders, according to Badaracco, work patiently and inconspicuously for their organizations and the world. He labels these leaders "nonheroes."

Supervising Co-workers

Co-workers must be seen, listened to, understood, and respected. Not least, they require feedback that tells them how their managers evaluate their contribution. Co-workers want to know what they have done well and what they should do differently. Given the sensitivity of the manager-co-worker relationship, managers' capacity for empathy is on display in many situations. This display is a high-wire act, in which managers must balance expressions of sympathy and compassion with the issuance of demands and criticism.

Managers must also allocate tasks among co-workers according to their skills and experience. It is a demanding task to combine logical reasoning with a warm and caring attitude when making such allocations. One must tread carefully as one encourages some co-workers and discourage others. Some co-workers may fiercely resent their assignments or re-assignments. Then, it is easy as a manager to become either too protective or too aggressive. In both instances, as conflicts over task responsibility flare up, co-worker morale may suffer.

Managing Change

Organizations must determine the source and intention of its change initiatives when they are first proposed. How were such initiatives proposed? Do the proposed initiatives support the organization's purpose and advance its goals? Change initiatives must be perceived as legitimate and meaningful as far as their intended future effect on the organization. Lacking legitimacy and purpose, it is unlikely that change initiatives will have the support of managers and co-workers who have the task of implementing them.

Organizational change that results in, for example, transformations in policy, structure, technology use, and leadership is not uncommon at organizations, large and small. We read nearly every day about reorganization, restructuring, mergers, and acquisitions in the business world. They are normal events in many work contexts. For managers, such events may present very challenging scenarios – even when the changes are well-motivated and welcomed.

To manage change successfully, managers must be good listeners. They must also have enough self-confidence and patience to tolerate co-workers' criticism and resistance. Rare is the change that is immediately welcomed by all involved. It is human nature to be wary of the new and unknown; hence, the survival of the species theory. Therefore, managers who understand that most people find change difficult will introduce changes with great sensitivity. If managers also have doubts about the changes, it may be a good idea for them to discuss the presentation of changes with someone they trust. In such a dialogue, an alternative way of approaching the situation may emerge.

For managers, the challenge is to take a long-term view of the positive aspects of the change. They may also need to exhibit principled courage when they question some change directives from top management. Managers must protect their work groups, especially in times of potentially disruptive change if they wish to retain the trust of their co-workers. Even with co-workers' support, managers may find themselves rather isolated if they question decisions made by top management. Of course, managers can only do so much. It is essential to bear in mind that the purpose of managerial resistance is not to cause trouble or conflict but rather to facilitate the accomplishment of the organization's goals and overarching purpose.

A commonly held idea in work life is that managers and co-workers must show unwavering loyalty to their superiors in the organization. Perhaps this idea depends on how loyalty is defined. If loyalty means people must betray personal ethics and principles to satisfy people in superior positions, this understanding of loyalty is quite dangerous. Just as elected officials swear or affirm their loyalty to constitutions – not to other elected officials – managers and co-workers owe their loyalty to their organizations' values and purpose, not to others in the organizational hierarchy (see Chap. 8).

It is easier to be a manager of a group that is characterized by openness and trust. The challenge in the managerial role is to maintain one's own integrity and to resist the temptation of groupthink (see Chap. 6). Groupthink is often a temptation when a work group is led by a manager who is idealized. Sometimes managers should also be prepared to accept a certain amount of envy and even subversion from manager colleagues who may resent the competition from a well-functioning work group. Such resentment is not uncommon if their own work groups have problems with cooperation.

Delegating

When the group is "in work" (see Chap. 6), leadership is delegated to work groups with the most competent group members leading the delegated tasks. The immediate challenge for managers at this point is to let group members lead. Rather than thinking they are no longer of use, managers should then seize the opportunity to rethink their work. Because they have coordinated the delegation of tasks, managers are invested in its success. After the delegation, they must ensure that work conditions are good, the work climate is positive, and resources are sufficient. We have observed well-functioning work groups that have been undermined by top management's perception that the groups are so efficient that they are probably over staffed. However, when staff was reduced, the groups were unable to achieve their goals. In such situations, managers must protect the work groups. This is no time for budget cuts.

As a manager, if you are doubtful that your work group has reached that level of maturity (where delegation is possible) or is not interested enough to take on leadership responsibility and control, it is time to begin a discussion with them. You and your co-workers can discuss whether the delegation of tasks is a good idea at this time, which tasks might be delegated, and how the delegation process might work. Do members have enough knowledge and experience to assume leadership roles?

Are they sufficiently enthusiastic about the roles? Will the manager continue to provide support if needed?

Under the general topic of shared leadership, researchers have studied how people share control (see Chap. 3). According to this research, the manager's primary task in shared or distributed leadership is to support and encourage the co-workers who lead subprocesses. In this role, the manager, who again acts as a catalyst for others' actions, ceases to be a problem solver for the group. As a manager, you can provide the time and space for your co-workers to learn how to manage the new responsibility (and related stress) of leading other people. You must also recognize, understand, and manage your own and your co-workers' anxieties and other emotions that result from leadership delegation.

Let us now turn to the "how" in the model and discuss leadership in action in more detail (Fig. 7.1, the columns of the grid).

Be a Role Model

Managers should set an example that inspires others to follow their ethical principles and democratic values. Setting an example means inspiring good behavior – respecting co-workers, taking responsibility, and demonstrating loyalty to the organization's vision and goals. Co-workers expect their managers "to walk the talk" – that is, to stand up for their principles and values, especially in challenging situations when others oppose them. Co-workers also expect managers to make and support decisions even when these decisions are controversial and require compromises. Managers should always support systems and structures in the organization that invite co-workers' participation and reflection.

Show Consideration

This requirement refers to managerial support for and interest in their co-workers. Managers, especially first-line managers, sometimes testify about the disproportionate amount of time they spend listening to co-workers' personal problems. But managers are not therapists. They can, however, provide a sympathetic ear and offer the support authorized by their organization's rules and policies. Consideration is about showing concern for co-workers openly and honestly – within the boundaries of the manager-co-worker relationship set by the organization. Showing consideration is about confronting co-workers directly and clearly when problems arise and expressing satisfaction for successful accomplishments. In manager-co-worker dialogue, expectations can be communicated and reactions from co-workers can be noted. From a theoretical perspective, it is interesting to observe that we expect leaders to be effective, clear communicators (which requires extraversion) and at the same time to be empathic, attentive listeners (which requires introspection and introversion).

Contribute to Meaning and Coherence

Managers can contribute to meaning and coherence by inviting co-workers to participate in decision-making and by providing conditions favorable to such co-worker participation. To that end, managers should communicate organizational purpose, goals, policies, and methods to co-workers. They should delegate responsibility and control as appropriate. When co-workers understand the meaning of organizational purpose and goals, special motivational measures are rarely needed. By this action, managers show they recognize the value that co-workers add to the organization: managers trust them, respect them, and need them.

Managers can always try compel co-workers to take certain actions against their will. However, if managers have the trust of co-workers, such coercion or manipulation is not needed. One may conclude in such situations that co-workers have delegated power and influence back to their managers. As a result, both managers and co-workers then contribute to the organization (Larsson et al., 2005).

How Can Group Processes Be Understood in the Light of MLG?

In the first work group development stage of *dependence and inclusion* (see Chap. 6), managers have most of the responsibility for the creation of group structure. *Managing day-to-day operations* (first row in MLG) will consume a large part of the manager's work in a less mature group. In this phase of group development, a manager has direct power to influence, which might be attractive and tempting for some. In building group structure, managers face dilemmas of the kind we have described in this chapter. In making controversial, possibly ethically or legally, ambiguous decisions, managers must "do the right thing" – and be seen to do the right thing. Taking responsibility may involve risk; not taking responsibility may pose an even greater risk.

The idea that managers are fit to *supervise their co-workers* (second row in MLG) assumes they know their co-workers' strengths and weaknesses. For example, managers need to know how well work group members can perform a shared task. Managers accept as inevitable that co-workers' conflicts sometimes will arise in such tasks. They also know they must resolve such conflicts. These situations are challenging for managers when they occur in the second work group development stage of *counter-dependence and fight* (see Chap. 6). In this stage, managers must clarify the co-workers' responsibilities in their shared tasks as they try to resolve these conflicts. Of course, it is not always easy to determine why a work group enters this stage as power gradually and partially passes from managers to co-workers. Therefore, it is essential that managers investigate the causes of conflicts as sensitively as possible. Are co-workers fighting over values, procedures, or work responsibilities? Have they (the managers), either by interference or neglect, provided the metaphorical tinder that ignited the blaze?

The need for clear confirmation or honest confrontation is greater in the first work group development stages. But good managers are attuned to co-workers' need for feedback in all work group development stages.

Some managers seem to enjoy a dynamic workplace with its co-worker conflicts, while others are very concerned when co-workers fight. Managers who are stimulated by excitement, tension, and conflicts might benefit from conversation partners who can dampen their impulse to enflame such situations. Managers who worry over co-workers' conflicts might benefit from conflict resolution training. It is necessary, however, for all managers to maintain some distance from the rights and wrongs of co-workers' conflicts. These conflicts should not become "the tail that wags the dog." Every manager's primary obligation is to the organization's goals and purpose.

To *manage change* (third row in MLG) when the work group's maturity is low may tempt you to introduce somewhat authoritarian solutions. However, such solutions, which typically are enforced by the threat of retaliation if co-workers take adverse actions, are never good for an organization (Edmondson, 2018). If a group is still dependent on its manager for direction and control, co-workers may respond passively to the change, or they may stubbornly resist it. No one is satisfied, including managers, if they must force acceptance of a change despite co-workers' passivity or resistance and, typically, despite union opposition if co-workers are unionized. Gradually, however, the change is implemented. The co-workers who most resist the change may not embrace it, but they may grudgingly accept it. Working with a group stuck in dependency is frustrating. Such work drains one's energy and presents a considerable obstacle to change.

If the co-workers as a group are already in conflict over some issue or problem when the change initiative is proposed or announced, their resistance to the change may increase. They may argue about the change openly if management does not discourage free expression at work. Ultimately, depending on how transparent the change process is, co-workers may agree to move forward with the change or not. As a group, they may regress in their development when they refuse to accept the change. The latter outcome is possible if management forces the change upon co-workers by manipulative means or if management stifles co-worker opposition. However, if management allows criticism and welcomes open discussions, trust will develop between managers and co-workers. The process will thereby contribute to the progression of the group into a more mature stage.

In general, the chance of success with a change is greatest if the work group is in the third or fourth group development stage: "trust and structure" and "work and productivity," respectively (see Chap. 6). In these stages, the group members have resolved their conflicts, they trust each other, and they have a clear grasp of their roles, tasks, and goals.

Delegation of responsibility and control, which begins in the third stage of group development ("trust and structure"), continues in the fourth stage ("work and productivity") (see Chap. 6). Managers who assign responsibility and control to their co-workers may find delegating one of their most challenging leadership tasks. It is a delicate task to decide when the group is ready for this step. We caution that some work groups do not respond well to delegation of responsibilities and control.

However, when work groups are ready, delegation is a rewarding experience for managers, if they understand that delegation means that co-workers may be more qualified by their knowledge and experience to manage certain tasks than their managers.

In the mature group development stages, work groups are willing to take responsibility for their delegated tasks and are prepared to lead when, for example, group members perform a shared task. Managers who resist delegating responsibility and control may hinder not only the group work but also the group development. In fact, the group's work and development both benefit if managers voluntarily yield some of their authority. Paradoxically, the manager's organizational position may strengthen if top management notes an increase in the work group's productivity and profitability after management delegation.

Indirect Leadership and the Creation of Trust

Top management supervises the higher-level managers who supervise the mid-level managers who supervise the co-workers. However, the management of managers (i.e., indirect leadership) is somewhat different from the management of co-workers (i.e., direct leadership), although management groups have the same group dynamics as other work groups (Larsson et al., 2005). Because managerial responsibility is different in degree of human relations involved compared to co-worker responsibility, managers must take even more time for self-examination and ethical reflection than the people they manage. With self-knowledge, combined with a general knowledge of humanity and society, managers can build trust in their organizations and in themselves by their actions and by their general presence – as revealed in their "way of being." For example, in their interactions with others at work, managers can build internal (personal) trust; in their public appearances and statements, they can build external (organizational) trust.

Trust, as organization researchers use this word, is not a capital asset listed on organizations' balance sheets. Trust is not quantifiable in the ways that accountants and auditors use to compute financial capital that is the result of verifiable transactions. Organizational trust is created, for example, by organizations' networks, reputations, and norms. Manager-co-worker trust is created, for example, by openness, reliability, and predictability in work relationships. Organizational trust and manager-co-worker trust are valuable intangible assets because of the confidence they provoke in others (Edmondson, 2018).

If mid-level managers do not trust their higher-level managers, they are disinclined to submit to their authority. In this unfortunate situation, mid-level managers may begin to set their own work priorities. They may think they should decide unilaterally what should be done and how it is best done. If top management is threatened by this loss of control, a harsh crackdown is likely. This is not a positive outcome for anyone. It is costly for organizations when people pull in different directions. The best solution, as Jaques (1996) writes, is to create commitment through trust that grows naturally from functional organizational structure, prudent distribution of resources, and managerial reliability.

To Be Anchored in Oneself

In his book, *Questions of Character: Illuminating the Heart of Leadership Through Literature*, Joseph Badaracco (2006) argues that leaders can learn more from stories in classic literature than from case studies set in the workplace. Leaders are repeatedly tested by challenges to their values, sense of responsibility, and principled courage – the challenges fictional character often face in literature. Badaracco concludes these challenges, when met and conquered, can reveal self-knowledge and insights that are essential for good leadership. He argues that success and failure in business have less to do with skills, merit, new technologies, social networks, or even experience than with knowing yourself. This self-knowledge, based on a realistic view of yourself and other people, helps leaders take responsibility and control at work and live a productive and meaningful life away from work.

When you begin your self-knowledge journey by asking yourself "who you are" and "what you want from life," you have set a course for life. This is as true in your professional life as in your personal life. If you trust your inner compass, you will gain confidence in yourself and in your work. Like dancers or skaters who perform with ease and confidence when they trust their partners on the stage or on the ice, as a manager you can relax and enjoy your work if you know and are grounded in yourself and have the trust of others.

References

Alvesson, M. (2017). *Reflexive leadership. Organising in an imperfect world.* Sage.

Alvesson, M., & Sveningsson, S. (2003). Managers doing leadership: The extra-Ordinarization of the mundane. *Human Relations, 56*(12), 1435–1459. https://doi.org/10.1177/00187267035612001

Avolio, B. J., & Gardner, W. L. (2005). Authentic leadership development: Getting to the root of positive forms of leadership. *Leadership Quarterly, 16*, 315–338.

Badaracco, J. L. (2002). *Leading quietly. An unorthodox guide to doing the right thing*. Harvard Business School Press.

Badaracco, J. L. (2006). *Questions of character. Illuminating the heart of leadership through literature*. Harvard Business School Press.

Bernin, P., & Theorell, T. (2001). Demand-control-support among female and male managers in eight Swedish companies. *Stress and Health, 17*, 231–243.

Carlson, S. (1951). *Executive behavior: A study of the workload and the working methods of managing directors*. Arno Press.

Collins, J. (2001). *Good to great: Why some companies make the leap … and others don't*. Harper Business.

Conradie, C. S., van der Merwe Smit, E., & Malan, D. P. (2016). Corporate health and wellness and the financial bottom line: Evidence from South Africa. *Journal of Occupational and Environmental Medicine, 58*(2), e45.

Edmondson, A. C. (2018). *The fearless organization: Creating psychological safety in the workplace for learning, innovation, and growth*. Wiley.

Fabius, R., Thayer, R. D., Konicki, D. L., Yarborough, C. M., Peterson, K. W., Isaac, F., et al. (2013). The link between workforce health and safety and the health of the bottom line. *Journal of Occupational and Environmental Medicine, 55*(9), 993–1000.

Fabius, R., Loeppke, R. R., Hohn, T., Fabius, D., Eisenberg, B., Konicki, D. L., & Larson, P. (2016). Tracking the market performance of companies that integrate a culture of health and safety. *Journal of Occupational and Environmental Medicine, 58*(1), 3–8.

Fors Brandebo, M., & Alvinius, A. (2019). *Dark sides of organizational behavior and leadership*. IntechOpen. ISBN 9781789847505.

Grint, K. (2005). *Leadership: Limits and possibilities*. Palgrave.

Grossmeier, J., Fabius, R., Flynn, J. P., Noeldner, S. P., Fabius, D., Goetzel, R. Z., & Anderson, D. R. (2016). Linking workplace health promotion best practices and organizational financial performance. *Journal of Occupational and Environmental Medicine, 58*(1), 16–23.

Holmberg, I. (2012). Managerial leadership as event-driven improvisation. In S. Tengblad (Ed.), *The work of managers* (pp. 47–68). Oxford University Press.

Holmberg, I., & Tyrstrup, M. (2010). Well then – What now? An everyday approach to managerial leadership. *Leadership, 6*(4), 353–372. https://doi.org/10.1177/1742715010379306

Jackson, B., & Parry, K. (2008). *A very short, fairly interesting and reasonably cheap book about studying leadership*. Sage.

Jaques, E. (1996). *Requisite organization. A total system for effective managerial organization and managerial leadership for the 21st century*. Cason Hall.

Johansson, G., Sandahl, C., & Hasson, D. (2013). Role stress among first-line nurse managers and registered nurses – A comparative study. *Journal of Nursing Management, 21*, 449–458.

Karasek, R. A., & Theorell, T. (1992). *Healthy work stress, productivity, and the reconstruction of working life*. Basic Books. ISBN 9780465028979.

Larsson, M., & Lundholm, S. (2010). Leadership as work-embedded influence – A micro-discursive analysis of an everyday interaction in a bank. *Leadership, 6*(2), 159–184.

Larsson, M., & Lundholm, S. E. (2013). Talking work in a bank: A study of organizing properties of leadership in work interactions. *Human Relations, 66*(8), 1101–1129.

Larsson, G., Sjöberg, M., Vrbanjac, A., & Björkman, T. (2005). Indirect leadership in a military context: A qualitative study on how to do it. *Leadership & Organization Development Journal, 26*(3), 215–227.

Larsson, G., Lundin, J., & Zander, A. (2018). *The leadership model – The art of matching individual and organizational characteristics*. Studentlitteratur.

Lohela-Karlsson, M., Hagberg, J., & Bergström, G. (2015). Production loss among employees perceiving work environment problems. *International Archives of Occupational and Environmental Health, 88*(6), 769–777.

Lornudd, C., Tafvelin, S., von Thiele Schwarz, U., & Bergman, D. (2015). The mediating role of demand and control in the relationship between leadership behaviour and employee distress: A cross-sectional study. *International Journal of Nursing Studies, 52*(2), 543–554.

Mintzberg, H. (1973). *The nature of managerial work*. Harper & Row.

Nyberg, A. (2009). *The impact of managerial leadership on stress and health among employees*. Dissertation. Karolinska Institutet.

Nyberg, A., Alfredsson, L., Theorell, T., Westerlund, H., Vahtera, J., & Kivimäki, M. (2009). Managerial leadership and ischaemic heart disease among employees: the Swedish WOLF study. *Occupational and Environmental Medicine, 66*(1), 51–55.

Sandahl, C., Birgersson, E., Janson, H., Sundlin, A. L., & Åkerlund, M. (2004). Performance-based personality tests in the assessment and selection of managers. *Organisational Theory and Practice, 15*(1), 35–44.

Siegrist, J. (1996). Adverse health effects on high-effort/low-reward conditions. *Journal of Occupational Health Psychology, 1*, 27–41.

Skogstad, A., Aasland, M. S., Nielsen, M. B., Hetland, J., Matthiesen, S. B., & Einarsen, S. (2014a). The relative effects of constructive, laissez-faire, and tyrannical leadership on subordinate job satisfaction: Results from two prospective and representative studies. *Zeitschrift für Psychologie, 222*(4), 221.

Skogstad, A., Hetland, J., Glasø, L., & Einarsen, S. (2014b). Is avoidant leadership a root cause of subordinate stress? Longitudinal relationships between laissez-faire leadership and role ambiguity. *Work & Stress, 28*(4), 323–341.

Styhre, A. (2012a). Identification work in the construction industry. Ideal selves, project performance, and disidentification. *Leadership & Organization Development Journal, 33*(7), 632–645.

Styhre, A. (2012b). Leadership as muddling through: Site managers in the construction industry. In S. Tengblad (Ed.), *The work of managers. Towards a practice theory of management.* Oxford University Press.

Tengblad, S. (Ed.). (2012). *The work of managers. Towards a practice theory of management.* Oxford University Press.

Tyrstrup, M. (2006). *On the brink of failure: The art of impromptu action in everyday leadership.* Studentlitteratur. ISBN 9144046537.

Wahl, A. (2014). Male managers challenging and reinforcing the male norm in management. *NORA, Nordic Journal of Feminist and Gender Research, 22*(2), 131–146.

Weick, K. (1995). *Sensemaking in organizations*. Sage.

Woods, S., & West, M. A. (2019). *The psychology of work and organisations* (3rd ed.). Cengage Publishing.

How to Act Professionally in the Manager Role

8

Stay focused on the overall purpose of the organization.

In this chapter, we will build on two concepts *professionalism* and *role* in trying to approach what professionalism in the manager role can entail. We also present a model for managers on how they can take their role in a more professional way. The model can serve as a guide for managers (and their co-workers) to find the balance between sense and sensitivity (i.e., reason and emotion) at work and at the same time keeping personal ethics and their organization's overarching purpose in sight.

What Is Professionalism?

What professionalism means with respect to the managerial role is not self-evident. Existing descriptions are often general and vague and offer no actual guidance on how to take the manager role in a professional way. "Professionalism," which links to the history of the professions (Abbott, 1988), derives from the Latin *professio,* which translates as both "declaration" and "occupation." A profession is thus a "declared occupation." The classic professions (e.g., physician and lawyer) are based in their long, solid, and specialized education and training. Practitioners of the classic professions are viewed as experts in their fields. Society authenticates their right to practice by a licensing or authorization process that confirms their qualifications. This authentication gives such professionals exclusionary rights to practice their specialty. Through this authorized knowledge, they will also have power over others as their knowledge cannot be questioned – except by others who have the same knowledge, that is, by the profession itself.

The classic professions historically had an altruistic purpose. Those who practiced these professions were considered to do it for the good of mankind. People needed to be able to trust the professionals, because they were dependent on their

C. Sandahl, M. von Knorring, *Managing with Sense and Sensitivity*,
https://doi.org/10.1007/978-3-031-24109-3_8

expertise. Therefore, to ensure that trust was not misplaced, the professions also created ethical rules for their practitioners that were backed by systems that enforced compliance. In addition, the professions took control of education and training programs to ensure that the latest knowledge became available and passed on to practitioners. Furthermore, society enacted laws and regulations that governed the professions, including the right to revoke licenses and authorization if necessary. The purpose was to strengthen the citizens' trust in the professionals.

Professionalism, as a concept, thus means that professionals are expected to be current with specialized knowledge in their fields of expertise, obey applicable laws and regulations, and maintain high ethical standards. At a minimum, this is what professionalism requires. These items provide a starting point for approaching the importance of professionalism.

To this point, our discussion has addressed professionalism generally. But what does professionalism mean in a manager role? To be a manager is not a profession in the way that the medical and legal professions are. People in managerial roles are not required to have specialized education and training. Society-approved authorization or identification for managers is not required. Although some organizations have tailored managerial codes of ethics, most managers are bound only by their organization's general code of ethics and lack specific ethical rules and guidelines on how they should manage their work or their co-workers.

Thus, to examine how managers can take their manager role in a more professional way, we need to take a different perspective than that used by the classic professions. We need to explore the concept of "role" in the managerial context, not only with respect to how managers perform tasks and take responsibility but also with respect to how managers cope with emotionally challenging situations professionally and responsibly. In the next section, we begin with a theoretical discussion of "role" as traditionally understood. Then, we will show how an expanded view of the role concept, which also includes the purpose of the organization, can help us understand what professionalism in the managerial role – or the employee role for that matter – can mean (Newton et al., 2006; Reed, 2001; von Knorring, 2010; von Knorring et al., 2016).

Role: A Theoretical Perspective

Role is one of the most central theoretical concepts in social psychology, and there are several definitions. In everyday work contexts, role is sometimes equated with job description. A manager might be informed: "Your role in this organization is to …." However, defining role as a job description is too narrow because then role is viewed as prescriptive, static, and unilaterally imposed by people in the upper hierarchy. In practice, people rarely stick exactly to their organizational job descriptions. Sooner or later, individual priorities come into play, and independent decisions are necessary. A dynamic and changing world influences those priorities and decisions. Role, so understood, is a much broader concept than job description.

Another way to look at the concept of role to see it as synonymous with the expectations, formal or informal, of a person in a certain context. Now role becomes an assignment – from others or in interaction with others.

Some situations and events may activate behavior responses (patterns) in us that are typical or for which we have a certain predisposition. People are often labeled with descriptive names (i.e., nicknames) associated with characteristic behavior responses. In a new group, for example, people may be assigned – secretly or not – the role of "the chatty member", "the quiet member," or "the awkward member." Some psychological interpretations in organizational psychology assign archetypal names from fairy tales to roles such as "the king," "the princess," "the hero," "the wise old woman," "the witch," or "the clown." These archetypical patterns of behavior are identified as "deep roles" by Moxnes and Moxnes (2016) and illustrates the dramatic narrative associated with these roles. History, culture, context, task, and group member characteristics influence how these predetermined roles are assigned. It may be a provocative and amusing game to link group members with fairy tale characters. However, the players risk falling into the stereotype trap when they categorize people according to single personality traits.

Another problem with these predetermined role assignments is that people are somehow viewed as victims of circumstances and of their own subconscious. There is a risk that they lose their sense of agency. If the process of uncovering such "deep roles" is not managed with care and integrity, the role assignments may prevent development and maturity, both for the individual person and of the group they are part of. Many people have probably felt the discomfort of being assigned a role in a group that they do not like. When the assigned role is flattering or semi-flattering (e.g., "the fixer of everything" or "the informal leader"), people may be less annoyed. However, even in such cases, the assigned role eventually may seem cramped and unfair. In our experience, there is a risk that the assignment of "deep roles" eventually will become an obstacle both for the organization to reach its goals and for you as a person to develop in the profession. The result might be that you get stuck with a label, such as "the princess," which might be charming for a while, but difficult to wash away.

This criticism may also apply to the theory on team roles developed by Meredith Belbin, an English researcher and management consultant. Belbin's (2010) contribution to group theory is that diversity in team members' behavior is essential for the well-functioning team. Belbin developed a test for determining a person's principal function in a team. He identified nine key team roles that are found in successful teams although every team may not have people in all nine roles. He identified the following roles: resource investigator, teamworker, and coordinator (the social roles); plant, monitor evaluator, and specialist (the thinking roles); and shaper, implementer, and completer finisher (the action or task roles). The problem with his team role theory, however, is its assumption that people have a predisposition for one of these nine roles. Obviously, team members must take different roles. However, we have not found empirical evidence that supports the assumption that people have predispositions for specific, predefined roles.

The Possibility of Choice

Role expectations can be difficult to escape, for example, in a work group. Yet roles are hardly static. The more you know yourself and the more you understand which psychological roles likely match your talents or which roles group members are likely to assign to you, the better equipped you are to choose your role.

We often take different roles in different contexts. People who are withdrawn and quiet at work may be very jovial and talkative outside of work. They may be decisive at home in ways they would never dream of at work. Can people be so different at work and at home and still be true to themselves? The answer is that our personalities allow for many possibilities. Depending on the circumstances, we are quite capable of exhibiting different personalities without losing our fundamental and indivisible identity (Sundlin & Sundlin, 2014).

In fact, without conscious thought, we usually adapt our behavior to our surroundings. We interact quite differently with our partners and spouses than we do with our small children. We behave differently at holiday parties with friends than we do in work meetings with colleagues. Yet it does not occur to us that we "play" the different roles. We simply use different aspects of ourselves, depending on the situation and its demands. This is something we do spontaneously without conscious reflection. Our children and colleagues would see through us straight away if we were not authentic or used parts of ourselves that do not fit the purpose of the situation and the context in which we find ourselves.

Actors know this. When they act a role in a play, they must be authentic in each scene. It is not possible to "play" a role – not even in the theater. Actors must also have a great deal of self-knowledge. They often learn to recall personal experiences and the emotions associated with those experiences. In this way, they discover something within themselves that resonates with their roles. Yet herein lies an apparent paradox. The actor's self-image may conflict with that of the dramatic character portrayed. How, then, should actors be themselves and still convince the audience of the credibility of the play's characters? Great actors know the only solution is to dig deep into themselves until they find a hidden aspect of their personality that matches that of the character they play on stage. Circus clowns have the same problem. If they just "play" a clown-like behavior without conveying the idea that a clown is just a clown (i.e., sweet and fun), they will frighten children with their scary pranks and creepy costumes instead of delighting them. Managers, in the same way, must be true to themselves when they take their professional role.

The Role as a Self-Regulating Principle

In the rest of this chapter, we will introduce a different way of understanding role that is inspired by the work conducted by Bruce Reed (1920–2003) and his colleagues at the Grubb Institute of Behavioral Studies in London (Reed & Bazalgette, 2006). They describe the role as a regulatory principle within the self. In this interpretation, the role is treated as a concept that is closely associated with individual responsibility. Roles are not regarded as something that you are a victim of or something that you are assigned to, but something that you yourself have a responsibility to take and form. Managerial role-taking, then, is not a passive process merely influenced by others' expectations. How managers choose to take their role is instead an active process based on how you as a manager interpret the organization's purpose and the organizational resources that are available (von Knorring et al., 2016). With this approach, managers' decisions on how to act in each situation will be based on their own reflected experience and thus reflect both sense and sensitivity.

For example, in a family with children, the purpose is probably to raise the children so that they eventually will be able to have full and rich adult lives. Of course, a family also have other purposes, but the parental role takes its starting point in this overarching purpose. However, the specific aspects of the parental role continuously change. Children develop, and as life events, relationships, and interests influence children, the parents may have to abandon certain aspects of their parental role.

To be a dad to a 2-year-old is something completely different from being a dad to a 7-year-old or a 13-year-old. In a specific situation, one might suddenly realize that one needs to abandon a way of being which is associated with a way of viewing one's child. The child from yesterday has changed. In such moments, one can sometimes feel both frustration and sadness as a parent, or relief and joy, but such moments are always linked to a feeling – at least if you care about your child. Our point is that the parenting role, as well as the managerial role, is dynamic and needs to be changed and adapted to the prevailing situation, even if the overall purpose is the same.

It is like sailing. You cannot take only one compass reading on a voyage. Not seldom, the direction of the wind changes unexpectedly. Maybe you had hoped to reach the harbor soon, but now it will be considerably later. Maybe you are hungry and tired, but you need to control yourself, use your experience, and now decide to steer the boat in a completely different direction than you had intended when you planned the journey. Under current circumstances, it is the only way to reach the goal.

It's the same in a workplace. Taking your role demands continuous and dynamic work. Different aspects of the realities, including ethical concerns and one's own and others' emotions, must be considered as circumstances change. The managerial role as well as the co-worker role is as dynamic as the parental role or the sailor's role. In changing circumstances, you must adapt your role as you search for workable solutions while still focusing on your original purpose. Even if the new circumstances require urgent attention, you should resist knee-jerk reactions and instead should consider a range of responses. Role adaptation applies equally to the parent, the sailor, and the manager.

To summarize, the essence of being a professional manager, as in all occupations and professions, is about taking one's role. The role requires you to prioritize the organization's interests, in the service of its purpose, over your own desires, even as you admit the influence of your personal needs and emotions on your professional behavior. We believe that taking an active managerial role, with sense and sensitivity, is a key aspect of managerial professionalism.

From Being "in Person" to Being "in Role"

One may view role-taking, in simplified terms, as the transition from the private self (person) to the professional self (role). To be professional at work, one has to move from being oneself "in person" to being oneself "in role" (see Fig. 8.2).

What then does "in role" mean? In the1990s, Jean Hutton Reed (2000) and Bruce Reed (2001) at the Grubb Institute of Behavioral Studies, London, presented a model they created for professional role analysis, which we have adapted slightly, and refer to as the "Role model" (see Fig. 8.3). The model highlights the importance of being authentic in the role. It emphasizes the importance of building on your own reflected experience while focusing your behavior on serving the purpose of the organization.

The model integrates three experiential elements: (1) the system one is part of and its purpose, (2) oneself as a person with emotions and desires, and (3) the system's context which provides resources and the space to maneuver. The role is created where these elements overlap. Since the model was presented, it has been further developed in different ways, both by Reed and others. To make it as simple and useful as possible, we have chosen only to marginally change the original model.

When you use the model you must repeatedly ask the following question: How can I (as a person), with the resources that are available (the context), act in this work situation (the system) in a way that contributes to the organization's purpose?

The question may seem both daunting and encouraging. Few people wake each day thinking about their organization's purpose. Regardless of your position, as for example, a CEO of a listed company or unit manager of a hospital pediatric ward, you have your own interests, dreams, experiences, and emotions. These personal driving forces will of course always influence how you act at work. However, when faced with work realities, you have some emotional and cognitive work to do. You have to change your perspective from person to role. Even if you as a person always are at the core of the role, you need to discipline your behavior from being yourself in "person" to being yourself "in role" regardless of how the system's purpose is formulated it will always differ to some extent from one's own needs and desires. To be professional in one's role, one therefore must actively shift the focus from one's own private desires to the purpose of the system and discipline one's behavior accordingly.

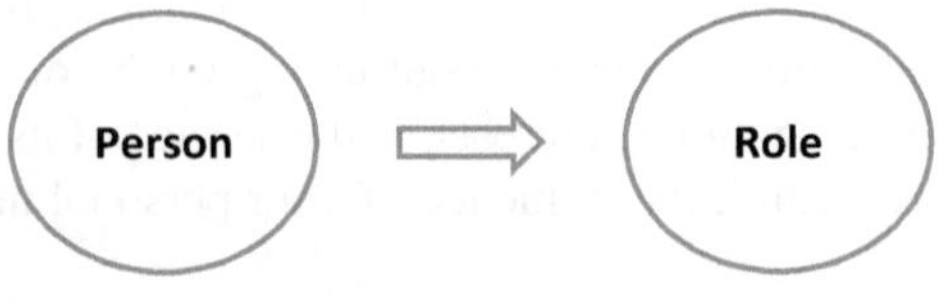

Fig. 8.2 Moving from being oneself "in person" to being oneself "in role" is a necessary transition for people in professional roles

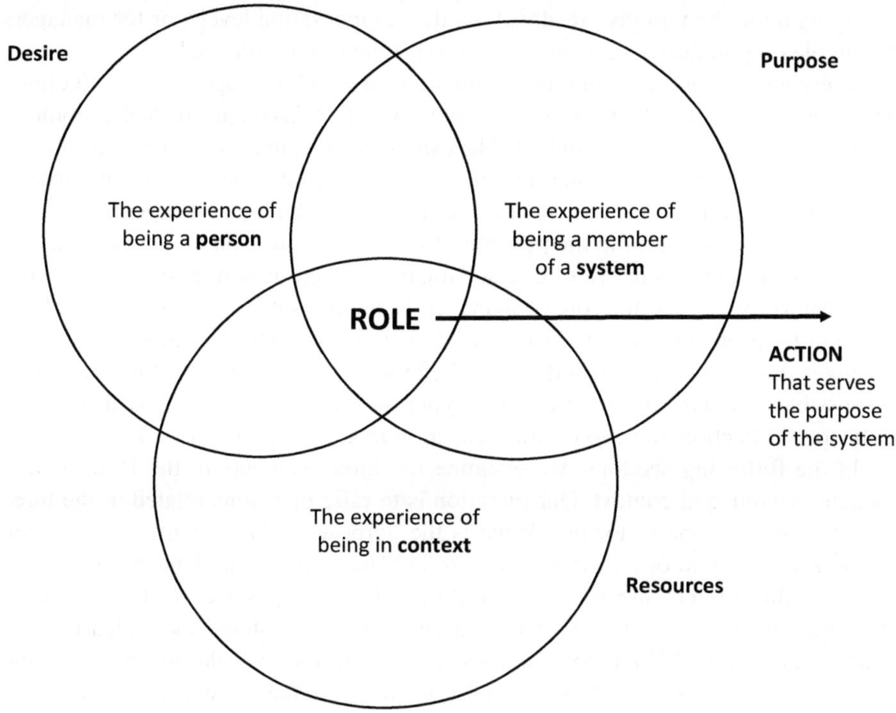

Fig. 8.3 The role model: A model for professional role-taking. (Adapted from Hutton, 2000; Reed, 2001; Reed & Bazalgette, 2006)

Without time for personal reflection on your personal desires in relation to the role and the system perspective, the risk is that personal desires will unconsciously influence professional behavior. You may find yourself acting "in person" rather than "in role" without your intention or awareness. Later in the chapter, we return to this risk.

Acting "in Role"

Acting "in role" does not mean, however, ignoring your emotions and desires. Nor does it mean avoiding evidence of compassion. However, in each situation, you have to decide which part of yourself to bring into "role" in order to support the system's purpose. When changing from being "in person" to being "in role," you use your experiences, emotions, and reasoning. Acting "in role," then, is acting with both sense and sensitivity.

However, it is often the case that being "in role" is less about how to act and more about how to refrain from action by exerting some self-control. For example, is it relevant for managers at co-workers' salary reviews to describe their sleepless night worrying about how to give feedback on the compensation levels, or for managers to ramble on pointlessly in meetings just to fill the room's silence?

These are only a few examples of situations in which managers may be inclined to say or do something that is more an expression of one's own needs in the moment, such as avoiding silences or conflict. The examples of situations can be made almost infinite, where you as a manager feel like doing something that may not contribute to the purpose of the organization or avoid doing something that is urgently needed. Which action contributes to the purpose of the organization, on the other hand, has no simple answer. There are of course situations where it is relevant to be deeply personal, or private, in the role of manager. Sometimes it is appropriate to exhibit anger or to respond with blunt firmness. After such incidents, it is important to have an inner dialogue with yourself as you reflect on your behavior. Otherwise, it is impossible to find the right expression of your person when "in role." We discuss the concepts "reflection on action" and "reflection in action" in the next chapter.

In the following sections, we examine the three elements in the Role model: system, person, and context. Our intention is to raise questions related to the three elements such as the following: What is the purpose of the system? How do you know which system or subsystem you are in? How can you understand that situations within different subsystems have different sub-purposes even if their overall purpose is the same? Is professionalism at risk when the system lacks a clearly communicated purpose? What are the consequences when you take too much or too little of your "person" into "role"? Finally, we focus on the context. Which laws and regulations govern the organization? Which resources are available? Which actions are possible when resources are scarce? We will show how managers in these situations need to keep these three aspects – the system, the person, and the context – actively present to act professionally in the manager role.

The System and Its Purpose

As we have pointed out above, the purpose of the system is central to being able to take one's role. However, we need to start examining what a system is, including its inner dynamic. The word "system" derives from the Greek word *systema*, which refers to a group of related entities that are arranged or compiled after certain principles. As used in this chapter, system relates to the so-called systems theory (von Bertalanffy, 1968). According to this theory, systems consist of, and can be part of, interdependent subsystems. Systems and subsystems can have a superior position, an inferior position, or an equal position relative to each other in a hierarchy. Whatever their position, they are still interdependent. An analogy is the cell in the human body. The cell is a part of an organ, which is a part of the body, which is a part of a social system (e.g., a work group).

To survive, a system must adapt to other systems or to their subsystems. Therefore, a system is in constant pursuit of dynamic equilibrium with its surroundings. This means that a change in a system, or in part of it, may immediately affect another system or systems, and vice versa. From systems theory, we learn that events that affect an entity or an individual are not always as they seem. You should always ask how occurrences in one part of a system link with the system as a whole or with other parts of that system. For example, a work group's hostile or indifferent atmosphere is not necessarily explainable by problems or conflicts within the group itself. Perhaps another work group, or a different organizational level, or even an external factor explains the work group's attitude.

To illustrate this point, we turn to the account of the offensive prisoner abuse and torture perpetrated by low-ranking US Army soldiers at the Abu Ghraib prison in the initial stages of the Iraq War in the early 2000s. Eleven soldiers were charged with various crimes, and two soldiers received prison sentences. In his book, *The Lucifer Effect: Understanding How Good People Turn Evil*, Philip Zimbardo (2008) describes his extensive research on the psychological and sociological factors behind immoral actions. Zimbardo convincingly argues that people's brutal acts, such as those at the Abu Ghraib prison, are rarely the result of individual factors alone; rather, such brutality is better understood as an effect of the systems people find themselves in. He concludes that the dark side of human nature is often revealed in inhumanely constructed systems that tacitly approve immoral acts in which "the ends justify the means" is offered as an excuse. A similar analysis can be applied to the cruel atrocities committed by the Russian Army in its invasion of Ukraine in 2022. Zimbardo warns that in other kinds of systems (e.g., organization and company systems), care must be taken that the means do not become the ends.

The idea that things are not always as they seem also applies to the interactions among people in systems. Popular management courses offered in the early 2000s taught managers how to deal with so-called difficult people. Of course, the definition of a difficult person is problematic. A person who is considered problematic and troublesome at work may also in practice have become a carrier of emotions shared by many others in other parts of the system. Some people are sensitive to certain kinds of feelings. There could be, for example, diffuse feelings of anxiety about an impending reorganization somewhere in a system. People who repress their anxious feelings need to find a way to express them, even if not seldom indirectly. Probably most people, at one time or another, could be described as difficult even when they express and demonstrate emotions experienced by others in the same system. For example, everyone, not just the difficult person, may feel anxious when they hear that many people in their organization will lose their jobs in an upcoming restructuring. When an individual or individuals dare to voice this fear, they may be described as difficult.

A classic example is the scapegoat phenomenon in organizations (Agazarian et al., 2021).

The term "scapegoat" comes from the Bible. The sacrifice of the goat in the Biblical story can be seen as a cruel illustration of how a system can find ways to restore balance.

> And when he has made an end of atoning for the Holy Place and the tent of meeting and the altar, he shall present the live goat. Then Aaron shall lay both his hands on the head of the live goat and confess over it all the iniquities of the people of Israel, and all their

> transgressions, all their sins, putting them on the head of the goat, and sending it away into the wilderness by the hand of a man who is in readiness. The goat shall bear all their iniquities on itself to a remote area, and he shall let the goat go free in the wilderness. (*Leviticus* 16: 21–22)

According to the story, the scapegoat was randomly selected. And there is no doubt that the destiny of the goat was to die in desolation. People who are blamed (often unjustly) for some mistake or error in a system can be sent symbolically into the wilderness when others, for example, isolate them, shun them, or bully them. The others have transferred their guilt to the scapegoat (i.e., "the fall guy") and are now innocent. This is how the modern scapegoat phenomenon works in organizations.

When taking a system perspective of what happens in organizations, the conclusion may be that individual-related or group-related incidents are caused by problems in the system. One familiar analogy: If you have a mild stomach ache it might affect the entire body. Managers who examine the system when problems occur may find, for example, that very powerful and irrational phenomena crop up within and between work groups. If they have a systems perspective they will be less inclined to blame difficult people for mistakes and errors that are attributable to the system and act in a more professional way as a manager.

Let us now return to the Role model. That which ultimately defines the system, in this case your workplace, is always the overall purpose of the organization. Managers, however, frequently find themselves in situations that require behavioral adaptations to achieve situational purposes rather than organizational purposes. An example illustrates this idea. Just before a staff meeting is scheduled to end, someone asks an urgent question that is only distantly related to the meeting's agenda. Should you, as manager, respond at once (and possibly at length because the question is complex)? Or should you tell the entire staff you will respond later? The question – perhaps it relates to the organization's overall purpose – matters to you, but now your immediate concern is the subsystem. The overall purpose, for example, to contribute to the health of the population will not help you to take your role in a professional way in this situation. Instead, you need to quickly define for yourself what the purpose is of the subsystem you are in right now, that is, what is the purpose of this meeting.

Thus, different situations in the workplace can have their own purpose even if this purpose falls within the wider scope of the organization's overall purpose. Such situations can have their own systems – that is, subsystems. For example, the purpose of a staff party is to socialize, to have fun, and to strengthen a sense of belonging that in turn might facilitate cooperation among co-workers. The manager's small talk at such occasions is not remotely like their participation at staff meetings, although the organization's purpose remains the same, regardless of the subsystem venue.

Managers, nevertheless, must always keep in mind the overall organizational purpose – even in situations when they need to adapt their behavior to achieve a subsystem purpose. That is their professional responsibility. However, if the overall organizational purpose is unclear, or even nonexistent – not an uncommon situation at many organizations – managers cannot act professionally in their role. Lacking a well-defined and accepted overall organizational purpose, being "in role" is a near impossibility for all involved, as there is no system with clear boundaries to take a role in, according to the model. Ambitious managers or co-workers often try to fill the gap themselves as they search for organizational purpose despite the risk that a mixture of purposes will create general confusion for everyone.

When there is no well-defined and accepted overall organizational purpose, people are inclined to create their own meaning and purpose. Then, there is a risk that informal forces replace formal governance structures and organizational chaos threatens. Managers and co-workers who try to bring order out of chaos by acting professionally become frustrated and exhausted, even defiant, if their efforts fail. No matter how you try, it is not possible to take a professional role at work if the organization lacks a system, as defined here with a clear purpose. Eventually you might be regarded as troublesome and disloyal; you may even become the scapegoat. In an organization where loyalty to the boss is more important than loyalty to the system's purpose, it is not difficult to understand why some managers are rewarded with promotions and bonuses for their individualism while others are not. If situations such as the one described above are repeated while you as manager lack the power to exert your influence, the wisest action may be to leave the organization, not least to protect your own well-being.

What Is an Overall Organizational Purpose?

Purpose is often confused with goal. Most organizations have goals that are designed to be achievable and measurable. However, organizational goals don't always relate to a clear organizational purpose. Purpose gives meaning to goals and is the "the goal of goals," that is, the end-goal. Purpose explains why actions are taken.

Consider the following example. A pharmaceutical company manager described the company's purpose at a joint planning day with the sales group in attendance. He began with this PowerPoint slide that was intended to inspire everyone in their daily work:

Our Purpose:

- To increase sales activities with 20 phone calls and three customers visits per week,
- To become the best in Sweden.
- To grow and employ five more people.

Was this an inspirational description of organizational purpose? Possibly it was for the most competitive salespeople in the group. For others, the response was likely less inspirational. Is the company's purpose simply greater growth, more sales, and (vaguely) "to become the best in Sweden"? Are these the reasons people work Monday through Friday, 8 to 5, week after week? Perhaps a more inspirational message might have touched on what the company stands for, the societal contributions it makes, the services it provides to customers, and the commitment it makes to the people it employs. Specifically, the manager might have highlighted the research that showed that one of its products decreased premature death in the population. Saving lives seems a more inspirational purpose than increasing sales.

An organizational purpose cannot be just elegant words, however. It must speak to people's fundamental values, principles, and passions. It must prove to people that the time and effort they spend at work has meaning beyond the company's "bottom line." A purpose explains to people why they do what they do. And it must inspire them to do it. A well-formulated purpose gives an answer to the question what the business is for – and why you are prepared to give a large part of your life to it. Therefore, work is sometimes a matter of life and death. Therefore, work is about ethics and morale, about taking a stand. Therefore, our emotions are easily aroused and gain power over us at work.

The Person and Its Desires

Let us now return to the Role model. Person in the model relates to our desires. Desires merit our attention, because they can be destructive as well as constructive. Our individual personalities make up "the person" and each of us is shaped by our personal desires. Not only are we different from each other, we ourselves exhibit different aspects of our personalities at different times and places. Some days we want to be the center of attention; other days we try to avoid drawing attention to ourselves. Some days we imagine taking charge at work; other days we would rather just stay home. Sometimes we feel supported by our colleagues; other times we may feel betrayed by them. The emotions stimulated by our desires are numerous and complex – anger, grief, envy, joy, shame, pride – the list goes on.

However, to act out one's feelings and private driving forces at work, that is, to be too much "in person," is not professional. When managers are too much "in person," they become unpredictable for the co-workers. Their actions may create all kinds of work problems. For example, co-workers might become confused or frustrated by the unpredictability of managers who are acting to satisfy their personal desires. In such situations, the manager's agenda (i.e., desires) may introduce an informal purpose that exists in parallel with the organization's formal purpose. If these purposes take different directions, the organization is at existential risk.

However, we caution that the pendulum can swing too far the other way. A manager with an attitude of being completely »rational« and only working for the purpose of the organization can become problematic and, in fact, unprofessional. Managers cannot, and should not, completely ignore their desires and suppress their emotions. Such a response can be both dangerous and unconstructive. It is because of our sensitivity as persons we have the capacity to respond to our co-workers' nonverbal signal as well as their verbal expressions. Only then, their feelings and experiences can resonate with ourown feelings and experiences. Without this resonance, we lack the empathy and compassion needed to create social trust. If managers act without access to the feelings and experiences attributable to their "person," they risk becoming contributors to emotionally impoverished, indifferent, and technocratic organizations. It is psychologically exhausting for everyone at work if emotions are swept under the rug, and empathy and compassion are absent.

Ethical Evaluation of the System's Purpose

Also, it is only as presons that we can ethically evaluate the system's purpose. When managers in a system take no responsibility for evaluating the purpose of that system, irreparable damage may result – to the organization and, in the worst-case scenario, to society. The following example makes this point.

In 1961, the American social-psychologist, Stanley Milgram (1933–1984), conducted a series of classic obedience experiments (Milgram, 1974). His research is still cited as among the most important obedience studies ever conducted. His results illustrate what can happen when people do not evaluate the purpose of a system.

Milgram used two groups ("teachers" and" learners") in his experiment that was designed to test the effect of punishment on learning ability. The teachers, who posed questions to the learners, administered a series of increasingly severe electric shocks to the learners when the learners gave incorrect answers to questions. The teachers were unaware that the shocks were not real. Teachers and learners could hear each other, although they could not see each other. As the shocks increased in intensity – in fact, a meter registered (falsely) the most intense shocks as lethal – the learners (who had been coached) screamed louder and louder. An "experimenter" encouraged the teachers to continue the experiment – despite the learners' screams – as the voltage increased to lethal levels. One-third of the teachers refused to follow that instruction because of their discomfort and horror. Thus, two-thirds of the teachers obediently followed the instruction.

Nearly 50 years after Milgram's experiment, Jerry Burger (2009), an American psychologist, partially replicated the Milgram obedience study (again, no actual electric shocks were administered). Burger found the obedience rate in his experiment was only slightly lower than in Milgram's experiment. Somewhat less than one-third of the participants in the Burger experiment refused to continue the electric shock procedure.

Milgram's and Burger's experiments reveal how we, as individuals in a system, should always evaluate the system's purpose when our principles and values are at stake. It is only as persons, as moral subjects (Bauman, 2020), that we can refuse to act contrary to our conscience. It is worth noticing that quite a few people refused to follow the autocratic rules of the experiment. As a manager, it is crucial to reinforce the emergence of such brave behaviors and to foster a culture of psychological safety (see Chap. 5), which supports open reflection on all kinds of possibly conflictual issues, including goals and purpose (Edmondson, 2018; Zimbardo, 2008).

The Context and the Resources Available

The last aspect of the role model is context, which relates to the resources that are available. Context refers to the surrounding systems of internal resources, as diverse as organizational budgets, frameworks, cultures, and people, and to external resources, as diverse as laws and regulations, competitive forces, the labor market, and the economy. Context also refers to organizational systems for governance: how they are constructed, implemented, and evaluated and how they influence managers' activities (e.g., meetings and administrative tasks,). An analysis of context raises questions such as the following: Which resources are available? How favorable is the current environment for this activity or business? Has good use been made of the available resources? How do people outside our system view the outcome of our work? These are the questions that must be addressed when evaluating the short-term and long-term survival potential of the system a manager is held accountable for.

The lack of power that managers often experience when resources are inadequate or unavailable (or when they are overwhelmed with bureaucratic administrative chores) is understandable. It is arguable, however, that the deficiency of resources is not the manager's worst enemy or necessarily a primary threat to the achievement of the organization's purpose. Rather, the greatest danger is the powerlessness associated with the victim role that managers sometimes assume. Being a victim may, in a strange way feel somewhat satisfying, especially if you can share your feelings with others. One can join others in blaming the context (people, conditions, and events). This is a behavior that may offer temporary relief when people seek sympathy from others. Much time and effort can be wasted by managers in requesting additional staff, software updates, more office space, etcetera, if budgetary resources are simply unavailable. We do not claim that managers should not try to improve their context by requesting additional resources. However, resources are rarely sufficient. Being »in role« then means to try to contribute to the purpose of the organization with the resources you have at your disposal. Resources of all kinds should be used judiciously and economically. It is of course not professional to act as if the resources would be infinite, or larger than they really are. This certainly applies also to human resources, both the manager's own and the employees'.

There is however another question about the resource unavailability that is relevant to pose to yourself: Is it morally defensible for me as a person, given adverse conditions and limited resources, to try to achieve something that I judge is likely to fail? If conditions cannot be changed and additional resources cannot be acquired, it may be time to consider leaving the organization. To act professionally in the manager role does not leave room for clinging to your position and remain in the organization while complaining and undermining the work. In signing an employment contract, you have agreed to take responsibility and you have made a loyalty pledge. This commitment, as stated earlier, is sometimes misunderstood as a pledge of loyalty to others who have superior positions in the organizational hierarchy, when it is rather a pledge of loyalty to the organization and its purpose. Managers who cannot work for that purpose owing to adverse conditions and insufficient resources have a choice: to remain or to leave. If you decide to remain, you must work responsibly, as best you can. If you can't do that, you have a responsibility, not only to the organization and its members but also toward yourself, to use your skills and your passion in a different context. The risk of professional burnout is high when you stay in a context where you find no meaning.

Finding, Forming, and Taking a Role

We have now reviewed the three aspects of the role model. To take the role of manager, with the help of the model in a professional way, requires both courage, time for reflection, and energy. But taking the role also gives energy and job satisfaction, not only for you as the manager but also for the entire organization. A formalized way of working with role-taking based on the model is organizational role analysis (Newton et al., 2006).

Organizational role analysis can be compared to a kind of psychotherapy in your professional role. In training programs on role analysis, usually a consultant or supervisor guides and supports a manager or a group of managers in the process of role-taking. The managers may also practice their ability to "role-analyze" themselves. This process consists of three steps: finding, forming, and taking a role. Guided by these *three steps*, finding, forming and taking the role, we now address some questions managers should ask themselves when engaged in role analysis. (For a more detailed description of role analysis, see Reed & Bazalgette, 2006.)

Finding a role means identifying your inner point of departure that gives you the energy to act from. This requires consideration of how the three elements – system, person, and context – relate to your work situation. You might ask yourself the following questions:

- What is the real overall purpose of the organization, behind the written mission and vision statements?
- What do the formal and informal systems (and subsystems) look like? What is the nature of the power relationships? Where in the system do I place myself? Who else is in these systems? (A sketch of the systems in which you place yourself and other keypersons may be useful.)
- How can I contribute to the organization? Do I have valuable experience, knowledge, and skills that can contribute to the purpose of the organization? Are they required? Does the organization need my contribution?
- Which external factors affect the organization? What is the organizational context? What characterize the organization's social and cultural environment? Which personal resources do I have available? What is my mandate?

Questions such as these will help you discover if an organizational system with an overall purpose exists that you are prepared to take a role in.

Forming a role means analyzing your readiness to commit to work for the purpose of the organization. It is difficult to form a role in an organization with an overall purpose that you cannot support. If you are not committed to the organizational purpose, you are likely to feel alienated and unable to add value to the organization. You might ask yourself the following questions:

- Does my image of the organization correspond with that of others?
- Does my image match what I have observed? Is it realistic?
- Have my experience and background limited my understanding of the organization?

As these questions suggest, you are now reflecting on your strengths and weaknesses, your emotions, and your own desires. This is a reflective process that involves the whole person, intellectually and emotionally, in relation to the organization as a whole and to its purpose.

By the time you have found the role and have begun to form it, you are well on your way to taking the role. You have concluded you can make a positive contribution to the organization. You and the organization seem to be a mutually beneficial match. You are no longer troubled by insecurity and doubt; you are enthusiastic and optimistic. You think you are ready to act "in role." Your enthusiasm and optimism spread to your co-workers.

Taking a role means empowering yourself as a person. In taking your role with authority, you are contributing to a culture of personal responsibility and self-control rather than a culture of external demands and commands. Taking the role, however, is an ongoing process of sustained effort. You constantly, in every situation, need to discipline your behavior and ask yourself: "Which of my feelings belong to this particular situation?" "What is relevant and what should I simply leave out?" In this way, you will take and regain the role continuously as the situation and the conditions change.

Often it may be wise to find a conversation partner who will give you feedback on how well you manage to act "in role." However, with practice, you will become better at recognizing, problematizing, and reflecting on your own desires and your responses to them. You will return repeatedly to the question we posed earlier in the chapter: How can I (as a person), with the resources that are available (the context), act in this work situation (the system) in a way that contributes to the organization's purpose? As you seek to answer this question, you will strike the right balance between the use of sense and sensitivity in your leadership.

The Organization in the Mind

Despite the importance of an overall organizational purpose, which we have emphasized in this chapter, often organizations are not especially effective in explaining and/or communicating their purpose. Nevertheless, people in organizations generally have some idea of what their organizations stand for. They may have an image of what their organizations are, or could be, or should be. Most people agree that the one essential requirement is that the work in the organization should be meaningful – not only for themselves but also for others including society in general.

However, do people in organizations agree on the organizational image? Do they agree on what makes the work meaningful for them? For example, a city's plan to build a public transport system that is sustainable, well-run, accessible, affordable, and safe is an organizational purpose. However, for the employees, this plan does not necessarily contribute to their meaning of the work. On a personal level, Charlie might work to deal with the climate crisis, Benny to feed the children and Ann to get money to rebuild the kitchen.

Contrasting images of the organization and its purpose can be provocative and confusing, both for managers and their co-workers. People employed by schools or banks, for example, are quite clear about who they work for. However, if you ask them to describe their employers, they will probably describe the "school" or the "bank" very differently. Their images of these organizations are formed by images other than those presented in their employers' formal plans, performance review templates, or codes of ethics and conduct. In organizational psychology, these images of organizations and their purposes are sometimes referred to as the "organization in the mind" or "the organization within" (Armstrong, 2005; Hirschorn, 1998; Hutton, 2000).

The "organization in the mind" is created from everyone's images of tasks, roles, purpose, rituals, responsibilities, and skills and from how failures and success are managed. The organizational images are formed by unique and often emotional experiences with formal and informal roles, systems, functions, and relationships. The images are also influenced by individual experiences with organizational cooperation and power.

Small differences in people's images of an organization can create disharmony in relationships. Larger, more disparate differences can be very problematic, even dramatic. For example, satisfied co-workers' images of the organization are not the same as those of dissatisfied co-workers. Managers in organizations may also have different emotional (subconscious) conceptions of the "organization in the mind." If these conceptions are not discussed with others, consensus is unlikely, if not impossible, within work groups and across work groups. Performance in joint projects and in shared tasks suffers when conflicting images of the organization and its purpose exist.

As a manager, you may assume your co-workers share your image of the organization and its purpose. Because you are convinced your image is realistic, it seems self-evident that they would have the same image. That is rarely true. When managers learn their co-workers have quite a different image of the organization, they are puzzled and even annoyed. We have met managers who were extremely frustrated by such revelations. One manager complained: "I have spoken at meetings. I have written memos. I have emailed. I have asked others to talk about the matter. How can I make them understand? It is hopeless!" We think, in general, that poor communication styles, rather than insufficient information, explain why managers and co-workers have different organizational images.

Figure 8.4 illustrates how different images of an organization can affect communication. Two persons may use the same word but may have different, even conflicting, understandings of that word. It can be quite baffling to engage in a

Fig. 8.4 Are our images of the organization the same? (After Reed & Bazalgette, 2006)

conversation with someone only to discover gradually that you and the other party are talking about completely different topics or ideas. The images of the organization can differ because of individual experiences, emotions, and reflections. These influences help us form an image of the "organization in the mind". When managers try to communicate their image to others, they should also try to understand the images others have formed. Managers might ask their co-workers questions such as the following: How would you describe the purpose of this task? How would you describe the overall purpose? When these questions are addressed, it may be possible to reach a mutual image and understanding of the organization and its purpose.

The Emotional Experience of the Organization

To distinguish the conscious inner image of the organization from the less conscious image, the concept "institution in the mind" (Hutton, 2000) has been used. This concept represents the latter aspect (i.e., the pre- and unconscious aspects of the mind). The "organization in the mind" is, as mentioned above, about the conscious images of how, for example, tasks, roles, purpose, rituals, responsibilities, skills, failures, and success/failure appear and are managed in the organization. The "institution in the mind," on the other hand, is about how emotionally charged images such as values, beliefs, hopes, and ideals are connected to the organization. Sometimes, these images touch on deep, existential issues.

To illustrate, let us imagine a company founded by an individual who had a vision that was about something much more than just material values and goals. The founder had an idea that he or she believed in and hoped that it would contribute to other values than just profitability. Somehow, this vision, this something that was bigger than the founder as a person, was conveyed to others who were engaged in the project. The "great discovery," or the original idea, will often be recounted as part of the organization's history. As a manager you generally try to include some of this indefinite, but important, existential message. It will be the basis of the organizational memory that the founder and managers proudly treasure. Such stories, often with an existential core, are used to explain the company's purpose to its co-workers, its business partners, and society. This is an example of how "the institution in the mind" gives direction and meaning to work.

However, quite often one can find that people in leading positions at the same organization have very different values and emotional links to "the institution in the mind." If these leaders do not talk about and process their inner images and the deeper meaning of the organization's activities, the co-workers are likely to be confused. Perhaps they are less aware of the subconscious emotions that are not so easily observed. However, to function productively at work, managers should understand work relationships at both levels. The better they understand their own inner world, the better they can deal with the outer world. The "soft" values associated with emotions contain important information about oneself (the way of being) and about the organization. Although productivity ratios and profitability figures tell a story about an organization, that story alone may provide insufficient motivation for people who seek employment that gives their lives meaning.

Keep the Dialogue About Purpose and Meaning Alive

As an organization develops, it is essential to communicate the fundamental purpose to the various stakeholders. One of a manager's most important responsibilities is to initiate and sustain the dialogue about the organization's work purpose and meaning. The goal of this dialogue is not to harmonize people's various images of the organization and its purpose, which is probably impossible. Rather, the goal is to create a work environment, such that co-workers and managers can engage in a dialogue about the purpose and the meaning. A dialogue about these diverse images may produce a truer image of the organization as a whole and help identify the problems that need to be addressed.

In this chapter, we have referred, in different ways, to the meaning of being professional in the role of manager. However, there is also the golden rule, as we mentioned earlier in this book: "Be true to yourself." Although managers "take" roles, their professionalism should prevent them from "playing" roles that others quickly see through. In their organizational roles, authentic managers are aware of, and interested in, the interactions with their co-workers and that they have been correctly understood: Am I clear? Have I listened carefully? Are we building mutual trust? How will our way of communicating influence our cooperation? The answers to such questions are key to creating fearless and psychologically safe organizations (Edmondson, 2018).

We do not imply that you, as a manager, will always succeed in taking your role. Nor will you stay "in role" at all times; sometimes you will act "in person." Your emotions may triumph over your good sense – perhaps when you are overwhelmed by information, perhaps when a co-worker makes insolent remarks, or perhaps when top management abruptly dismisses your request for support. In such moments, you may feel anything but professional as you respond in a way that you might regret, perhaps in public. Despite your subsequent dismay at how you reacted, you may take some comfort knowing that every manager has had this experience – more than once. It is part of the role of manager to experience such unpleasant moments from time to time. The task then becomes to endure and try to remember the overall purpose and the purpose of the subsystem you are part of, until you feel safer. You should then take the time needed to return to "role" as you reflect on how you might handle a similar situation in the future. It is from such experiences that people develop – as persons and as managers.

References

Abbott, A. (1988). *The system of professions: An essay on the expert division of labor*. Chicago: Chicago UP.

Agazarian, Y. M., Gantt, S. P., & Carter, F. B. (2021). *Systems-centered training*. Routledge.

Armstrong, D. (2005). *Organization in the mind: Psychoanalysis, group relations and organizational consultancy*. Karnac.

Bauman, Z. (2020). Postmodern ethics. In *The new social theory reader* (pp. 138–145). Routledge.

Belbin, R. M. (2010). *Team roles at work* (2nd ed.). Routledge. ISBN 781856178006.

Burger, J. (2009). Replicating Milgram. Would people still obey today? *American Psychologist, 64*, 1–11.

Edmondson, A. C. (2018). *The fearless organization: Creating psychological safety in the workplace for learning, innovation, and growth*. Wiley.

Hirschorn, L. (1998). *The workplace within*. MIT Press.

Hutton, J. (2000). *Working with the concept of the organisation-in-the-mind*. The Grubb Institute.

Milgram, S. (1974). *Obedience to authority; an experimental view*. Harper Collins. ISBN 978-0-06-131983-9.

Moxnes, P., & Moxnes, A. (2016). Are we sucked into fairy tale roles? Role archetypes in imagination and organization. *Organization Studies, 37*(10), 1519–1539. https://doi.org/10.1177/0170840616634135

Newton, J., Long, S., & Sievers, B. (Eds.). (2006). *Coaching in depth. The organizational role analysis approach*. Karnac.

Reed, B. (2001). *An exploration of role*. London: The Grubb Institute.

Reed, B. D., & Bazalgette, J. L. (2006). Organisational role analysis at the Grubb Institute of Behavioural studies: Origins and development. In J. Newton, S. Long, & B. Sievers (Eds.), *Coaching in depth: The organisational role analysis approach*. Karnac.

Sundlin, A.-L., & Sundlin, P. (2014). *Taking up your role: How to shift between life and work without losing yourself.* Catalyst Communications Press.

von Bertalanffy, L. (1968). *General systems theory: Foundations, development, applications*. Braziller.

von Knorring, M. (2010). *The manager role in relation to the medical profession*. Dissertation. Karolinska institutet.

von Knorring, M., Alexandersson, K., & Eliasson, M. A. (2016). Healthcare managers' construction on the manager role in relation to the medical profession. *Journal of Health Organization and Management, 30*(3), 421–440.

Zimbardo, P. G. (2008). *The Lucifer effect: Understanding how good people turn evil*. Random House.

9 Developing as a Manager with Sense and Sensitivity

Without time for reflection, there is no learning.

In this chapter, we describe how you as a manager can use reflection in your daily activities to increase your knowledge and develop your competence. In this way, you develop as a manager with sense and sensitivity, that is, a manager who act using both reason and emotion.

Throughout this book, we have addressed the emotional challenges that confront managers daily. Most of the time, one must face them alone. While managers may respond differently to these challenges, each challenge is an opportunity to learn and develop.

The Importance of Reflection

Although we have not specifically emphasized the word "reflection" in previous chapters, we have urged managers to think about emotional challenges, the meaning of work, the importance of purpose, about group relationships and dynamics, and about personal responsibility, ethics, and professionalism. Why is such reflection important?

The word "reflection" derives from the Latin *reflectere*, which means to turn one's thoughts back, to analyze, to ponder, and to consider the past. We might turn our thoughts back to experiences already made, reflect on what is going on right now, or reflect on something that is planned to occur in the future. Whenever we do so, we have an opportunity to think and to learn. Reflection requires the courage to investigate and sometimes questioning one's own and others' motives and actions – not for the purpose of criticizing but to be able to act wiser and more appropriate next time.

When you create time and space for reflection in the workplace, you create the conditions needed for collective learning (Alvesson, 2016; Argyris, 1999;

C. Sandahl, M. von Knorring, *Managing with Sense and Sensitivity*, https://doi.org/10.1007/978-3-031-24109-3_9

Edmondson, 2012; Schön, 1983; Wilke, 2014). The knowledge that managers and others acquire through reflection can spread throughout the organization as organizational (or institutional) memory. Thus, the institution-created knowledge acquired through individual and joint reflection is not lost when people leave the organization. It is retained as a common knowledge, because it derives from shared reflections on shared experiences. It becomes part of the DNA of the organization as an institution.

A natural, and inevitable, part of shared reflection and dialogue is that differences of opinion will come to the fore. With an open mind, such conflicts can be contained and solved, unless they are antagonistic and related, for example, to power struggle, which is a more complicated situation. External help might be needed in such cases. However, most of the time, it is a matter of trying to *detect similarities in the apparently different and differences in the apparently similar* and to integrate differences into one's own thinking (Agazarian et al., 2021). The more differences you can integrate, the more complex your view of yourself and the world will become. As a result, you will be more fit to deal with the complexities of your daily life, because then your inner world corresponds better to the outer world. Daniel Siegel, a clinical professor of psychiatry and interpersonal neurobiology at the UCLA School of Medicine, argues that integration of such differences, through reflection and dialogue, is the key to well-being – that is, to acknowledge them and creating relationships within oneself and with others. He and many others have demonstrated that the development of neural connections in the brain are influenced by children's attachment to caregivers. We know that difficult, early relationships can result in problems with, for example, memory and emotional regulation. Research on child development and neurobiological studies of the brain have confirmed this linkage (Siegel, 2020).

Perhaps more interesting in the context of leadership is that studies of adults reveal that *relationships* with others *and reflections on relationships* are mirrored in your brain, in that it stimulates the integration of cells in the prefrontal cortex according to Siegel (2020). When these cells are integrated, they become more stable, and their connections become more complex. Increased complexity in the brain, which is related to increased complexity of the mind, increases the following human capacities and responses: adaptability to difficult situations, resilience, emotional competence, compassion, ability to cope with stress, and general health (Siegel, 2020).

According to interpersonal neurobiology, positive relationships, time for inner-world reflection, and verbalization of emotions promote healing and maturity as the mind develops throughout life (Siegel, 2020). Through dialogue and reflection, we can modify unconscious response patterns into constructive coping behaviors. However, time is needed for reflection and dialogue, valuable time that needs to be organized and planned, which we will return to later in this chapter.

Reflection Requires Courage

Like others, managers want to feel competent, that is, skilled in performing their various tasks, and be proud of themselves and their work. And, like others, managers are vulnerable and dependent on others. As we have explained in previous chapters, leadership often requires the courage to tackle head-on the many challenges this complex role poses. Inevitably, managers face challenges of many kinds in their work. Thus, courage is required when managers reflect on the causes and outcomes of the challenges that often arise from the vulnerability, dependence, and responsibility that are present in the role of manager. And sometimes one may need to move on, despite doubt, despite fear and a feeling of at least temporary loss of control.

Reflection means examining, even doubting, your own possibilities, limitations, and motives. It can even cause you to set aside your doubts, stop worrying about loss of control, and move on. In short, courageous managers use reflection as a tool for learning, evaluation, and decision-making.

When you feel vulnerable, as in situations when doubts are raised about your authority, competence, or judgement, it is a natural reaction to defend oneself – in various ways. You may project these doubts onto others or hide behind established preconceptions instead of admitting your own weaknesses. These defense mechanisms undermine your autonomy. However, autonomy is strengthened when you have the courage to reflect on your emotions, choices, and actions. These are the kind of situations when the manager's will and courage are tested.

Aristotle thought courage was the most important of all the virtues. He argued that courage is the mother of all virtues because without it, you cannot consistently perform the others. And courage develops, he argued, when you act courageously. The action is the manifestation of courage, or the lack of it. When you experience what happens and reflect on the consequences, you learn more about yourself and how you can act courageously and possibly ways you are using to avoid such situations. The American existential psychologist Rollo May (1909–1994) described two kinds of courage: moral courage and creative courage. Moral courage, he argued, is the righting of wrongs. In contrast, creative courage is the discovering of new forms, new symbols, and new patterns, on which a new society can be built (May, 1994).

People who exercise moral courage look back to discover what went wrong. Thus, reflection functions as quality assurance. People who exercise creative courage use their imaginations to build and develop. Thus, reflection functions as inspiration. Without reflection, it is difficult to correct our mistakes or to find opportunities for creation and renewal.

Reflection to examine the familiar, that which one takes for granted, is not always pleasant. When we reflect on our mistakes – our errors of omission and commission – in the moment we may feel embarrassed, ashamed, or guilty. The feedback one gets by reflecting, alone or with others, is often very true. That does not make it any less painful – maybe the other way around. That is why courage is needed.

Learning from Experience Through Reflection

Learning can of course be acquired more formally by "book learning" that is not based in direct experience. Such knowledge assimilates theoretical content, provides cognitive structure, and develops the language needed to describe experience.

David Kolb, an American professor of organizational behavior and development theorist, is one of several researchers who have studied the importance of reflection on organizational learning. Kolb based his theory of experiential learning on theories proposed by earlier philosophers, educators, and developmental psychologists (e.g., John Dewey, Jean Piaget, and Kurt Lewin). In his well-known "experiential learning cycle," Kolb presents four stages in the cycle: concrete experience, reflective experience, abstract conceptualization, and active experimentation. People learn as they move from experience to reflection to theory to experiment.

Figure 9.1 is our simplified version of Kolb's learning cycle that he later described as more an experiential learning spiral than a learning cycle (Kolb, 1984).

By reflecting on experiences, managers can create new knowledge and acquire new perspectives. If they simply repeat the same action again and again, without reflection and conceptualization, they will probably become more proficient. But what if that action is foolish or dangerous? Albert Einstein is often credited with defining stupidity as doing the same thing repeatedly and expecting a different result. The risk in skipping over reflection and conceptualization is that no learning takes place, and no quality assurance is conducted. In such cases, the probability of introducing systemic errors into the organization is high. Reflection on experiences (including emotions and ideas) can result in more thoughtful ways of acting. That is how we learn from experience.

People at work acquire actionable theoretical knowledge by testing new ways of acting in everyday processes and routines. As a familiar example, think about competitive swimmers. They practice the strokes and styles they have learned. As they

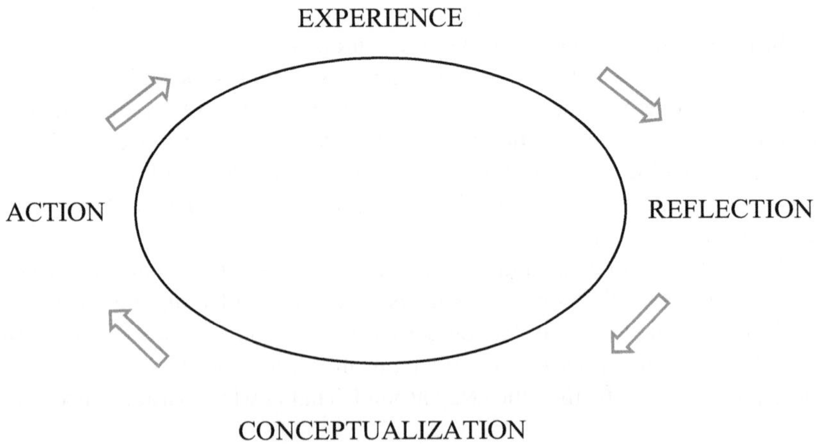

Fig. 9.1 Reflection on action. (Adjusted after Kolb, 1984)

practice, they reflect on their performance and evaluate the skills they have experimented with. In this way, they increase their knowledge of swimming. It is the same in the workplace. By reflecting on their work, managers can realize their theoretical knowledge in action. The entire work group is the beneficiary of this knowledge when improved ways of working remove unnecessary obstacles and advance the organization's purpose and goals.

The American philosopher Donald Schön (1930–1997) worked in the same spirit as Kolb and contributed to our knowledge about organizational learning and reflective practice. He differentiated between reflection *on* action and reflection *in* action (Schön, 1983). Reflection on action takes place after the event so to say, while reflection in action takes place while the event takes place. The latter is a somewhat more demanding practice. The more you get used to reflect on action, the more skilled you can become in reflecting in action, which requires a kind of split vision. You need to be present in the here and now as the event develops and at the same time find an inner room, where you can reflect about what is happening both in terms of emotions among the participants in the ongoing situation and the factual development of the subject matter. If you can develop this capacity, you will also find that your sense of timing will improve.

Developing Self-confidence and Self-esteem as a Manager

Before we continue to describe how to create space for reflection, we want to say a few words about how reflection can contribute to developing self-confidence and self-esteem in the role of manager. Self-confidence and self-esteem are sometimes used interchangeably, but they are not perfect synonyms. A main cause of high self-confidence is the mastery of some activity or skill. Self-confident managers know what to do in their areas of expertise and experience. However, high self-esteem is not guaranteed by high self-confidence. Self-esteem has more to do with who you are, how you feel about others, and how you feel about yourself. Despite managers' acknowledged expertise and relevant experience, their self-esteem can still be low. Past and present negative work (and nonwork) relationships and incidents can have damaging effects on self-esteem. Self-esteem affects managers' decision-making ability, either constructively or destructively, depending on how they feel about themselves. In the best of circumstances, managers' low self-esteem can recover over time.

If you act in a way that leads to the desired results, your experience of competence will be affected positively. This becomes particularly evident when the actions taken are in response to emotional challenges. To succeed because of one's professional expertise is of course good for self-confidence. However, the challenges in which self-confidence and self-esteem are at stake relate more to interpersonal relationships than to professional expertise issues.

It follows that managers' problem-solving and decision-making abilities will be negatively affected when they think they are not handling everyday activities well. It is inevitable at such times that their self-confidence and self-esteem diminish.

When managers discover that their decisions or actions were a mistake, they feel even worse. Unable to think clearly, they make more mistakes, so begins the downward spiral as they doubt themselves. Now more than ever, reflection within oneself and dialogue with others become indispensable tools for reversing this downward spiral.

Creating Space for Reflection

Unfortunately, few organizations create the metaphorical space that managers need for reflection, despite the lip service often paid by organizations to staff development. The explanation given, if any, is the lack of time. In our experience, time is not the issue. Rather, it is a matter of priorities. When organizations recognize the importance of workplace reflection, time is found for reflection. When conversations about emotions and ethics are not organizational priorities, the risk of organizational loss – in many forms – increases.

We have observed that experience-based learning acquired by reflection can produce new meeting routines, in which people's experiences and emotions can be expressed, heard, and dealt with. Although a forum for such reflection is essential, that alone is insufficient. Knowledge, legitimacy, and good role models are also needed. Managers need to provide opportunities for open discussion of what has been learned by reflection. We suggest, for example, that after task or project completion, and in some contexts at the end of the day, everyone involved should reflect jointly on the work completed together, positive and negative aspects of cooperation, pros and cons of plans, organization, and results. By highlighting each other's achievements, morale is bolstered for the next step. By airing co-workers' grievances, discontent may be avoided in the future.

Consider this analogy. If you do not want to explore feelings and concerns which are expressed by your co-workers and if you do not want to investigate their source, it is like turning off the smoke alarm without looking for the flames. Responding passively (or not at all) to signs of feelings of, for example, worry, sadness, anger, or frustration is a common temptation among managers – and among co-workers. It is difficult to put feelings into words. But that gives no reason to avoid them. Managers may think (and hope) the problem will just disappear given enough time. We think, on the contrary, that managers should explore expressions of emotions. To be able to learn from the emotions conveyed, time needs to be set aside either alone or with others. However, long periods of tranquility are not needed. Reflection can take place in the moments, the cracks which are opening during daily work, maybe a short lunch break on your own, or 10 min at the end of the day before leaving the office, or on your way home. Maybe, you want, like Marcus Aurelius, the Roman emperor, to spend a few minutes now and then to put your reflections into writing (Badaraccco, 2020). To encounter real situations while the work is in progress provides opportunities to develop and learn as a manager, and one will be better prepared to take thoughtful action in the situation in question.

Thus, reflection requires both mental and physical space. Managers may sit in their offices to reflect alone. Or they may reflect with the work group in the conference room. Maybe you will organize time together at the end of the day to go through what went well today, what could we have done better, what was difficult, etcetera. Or you may choose one option one week, and the other the next week. While there are no fixed rules about reflection space, we believe the ideal is to create routines for reflection in everyday life. As we have argued throughout this book, even the most successful managers are dependent on their co-workers. In your role as a manager, you need to consider how you work together, how you fail to cooperate, etcetera. On your own, you can only reach so far in your understanding of what is going on in your organization. However, together with all involved you will reach a mutual understanding that will guide further actions (Wilke, 2014).

For example, most managers, when preparing for a meeting, think the following: "Have I done enough preparation?" "Which agenda items should I prioritize?" "Which decisions should we make today?" Even during meetings, managers continue to reflect. When heated disagreements surface, they may think the following: "What is this argument about?" "Do people have hidden motives?" "How can I resolve this situation amicably?"

Reflection for managers does not end when meetings are over. Depending on how well the objectives of the meeting were achieved, additional reflection may be in order. In any case, managers should, at least, think about how they conducted the meeting. Managers may note what went well and what they would do differently at the next meeting.

At times, freer and more associative reflection is appropriate. In this kind of reflection, ideas and emotions are examined more spontaneously and more creatively. At other times, reflection should be more sensitive and more confidential. When conflicts exist among goals, values, and interests, systematic ethical reflection that addresses valuable perspectives and interest groups might be needed to improve the critical awareness of the values that lies behind choices people make in such situations. The research literature describes different specific methods that can be used for reflection (Badaracco, 2020; Branch & George, 2017).

We do not exaggerate when we say reflection space is probably among the least prioritized spaces in people's work lives and personal lives. People tend to minimize reflection just when thoughtful analysis of a situation, event, or relationship is most needed. For managers, perhaps a fierce competitor appears to challenge your organization's market share, or new health and safety laws are enacted; perhaps an epic product failure, or a cyberattack occurs. Although immediate action seems called for in such situations, we advise that knee-jerk responses are dangerous. To be blunt, it is just as stupid and short-sighted for the business to prioritize away the reflection space, especially in situations of lack of time and stress, as prioritizing away the jogging trip or the walk when you start to get back pain or aching shoulders. As with physical exercise, it requires practice, and with training, the results from reflection will come quickly. Badaracco's (2020) advice is to (1) aim for the good enough, (2) downshift occasionally, (3) ponder the tough issues, and (4) pause and measure up. Reflection is not about making things harder or more difficult. It is about trying to get it right. To rest, to look out through the window or to lie down in the grass in a summer day, is not a waste of time; it is about taking time to find out what needs to be done.

People who suffer from workplace stress – in periods of tight deadlines or heavy workloads – benefit from calm periods of reflection or relaxation. A walk in the park, 20 minutes of yoga, and a quiet conversation with a trusted colleague can all be more beneficial than working longer hours, skipping lunch, or taking work home.

Taking Responsibility for Ethical Actions

Reflection is a prerequisite for taking responsibility for organizational ethics (e.g., human dignity, equality, justice, and solidarity). For managers, this responsibility means actively and visibly supporting the organization's values and principles. This support requires managers to act with sense and sensibility. Managers examine questionable actions through an ethical lens, decide if the actions are socially rooted and organizationally approved, and determine if the actions comply with laws and regulations. They may ask themselves questions such as the following: "Are we allowed to do that?" "If yes, on what grounds?" "Which ethical values are at stake?" "Have we done the right thing in a principled way?" Such questions cause managers to focus on the sustainability of their organization, work environment, their own and their co-workers' future, social trust, and the common good.

Managers, as the guardians of organizations' ethical values and principles, should always be alert to threats posed by people with conflicting codes of conduct. In the worst case, these threats may appear as theft, bribes, extortion, conflicts of interest, embezzlement, or money laundering. Courage is needed to be able to motivate decisions with ethically sustainable arguments in such challenging situations. In addition, managers must reflect on the people, the events, and the circumstances. Why was the organization so vulnerable? Was there a systemic failure as well as a people failure? What remedies should be taken to prevent future incidents? In such cases reflection is required (Harris & Sandhu, 2017).

Managerial Supervision and Learning

Except for reflection and learning integrated in the daily work processes, different types of supervision can also support organizational learning. The role model introduced in Chap. 8 can serve as a useful point of departure for such supervision.

Supervision can be provided from outside coaches or consultants, but it can also be organized using resources within the organization or in collaboration with other organizations.

One example is to provide supervision at the group level. To develop as leaders, managers may meet with peers from other parts of the organization, or from other organizations in formal or informal settings. At such meetings, managers can discuss work problems and remedies. An external consultant, personnel from human resources or a senior colleague may chair the formal meetings. It is important that the leaders of such reflection groups do not have any formal or informal power in relation to the participants. As they exchange and discuss experiences, managers acquire learning they can apply in ways that connect their actions to the organization's purpose and intended outcomes. It is important that such supervision is task oriented and focused on real dilemmas or problems experienced by the participants in their daily work.

This kind of structured coaching is an example of an evaluated managerial method used in group supervision (Ladyshewsky, 2006, 2017). Evaluations of this approach have revealed that leaders, who receive such coaching, experience a more positive and effective leadership attitude. They are more focused on their leadership tasks and have more self-confidence in their ability to act. According to Palm et al. (2015), co-workers observed these same behavioral changes in their leaders who had received such coaching.

Developing Good Leadership

It is common that management courses take place outside the managers workplace, where the specific organization's governance systems, top management's demands for results, or co-workers' complaints is not present. Despite this, we believe it is important to attend such management courses, including reading the literature. In the same way, as it is a good idea to learn the theory of sailing before you practice sailing, it is an important step to become professional in the role of manager to learn theories and achieved knowledge of managerial leadership. However, our primary message in this book is that good leadership is based on authenticity, integrity, ethical considerations, and role-taking – all of which require that managers can be in touch with the emotional atmosphere at work as well as their own feelings, i.e., to be able to do emotional work and to use emotions as information (see Chap. 4).

Managers develop professionalism in the managerial role on the job – in practice, as they critically reflect on their leadership as it is and how it could improve. While they can always imagine what their responses might be in hypothetical situations, there is no substitute for real situations. No matter how well-prepared you think you are, you do not know how, with certainty, you will react in the moment. Managers require the emotional responsivity intelligence to understand and respond to others' needs and concerns in a professional manner – whatever the situation.

It may be as challenging to become a highly successful and respected manager as it is to become a well-known painter or a sports champion. In the art world and the sports world, training and focus, combined with energy and determination, are essential. Such high achievers also require constructive feedback. They need space to reflect on this feedback as well as on their experiences. They should think about what went well and what did not. It is the same for managers.

As a manager, you are expected to solve workplace problems – large and small, urgent, and routine. You also need to take care of employees as well as the business and other stakeholders such as customers or users. To do this with sense and sensitivity and in a respectful and nonauthoritarian way poses challenges also for the most reasonable and sensitive of managers. However, as we have argued in this book, if managers use the learning acquired thorough experience and reflection, they build a character and reputation that supports them as they search for solutions to the most difficult managerial leadership problems.

References

Agazarian, Y. M., Gantt, S. P., & Carter, F. B. (2021). *Systems-centered training: An illustrated guide for applying a theory of living human systems*. Routledge.

Alvesson, M. (2016). *Reflexive leadership. Organising in an imperfect world*. Sage.

Argyris, C. (1999). *On organizational learning*. Blackwell Business.

Badaracco, J. L. (2020). *Step back. How to bring the art of reflection into your busy life*. Harvard Business Review Press.

Branch, W. T., & George, M. (2017). Reflection-based learning for professional ethical formation. *AMA Journal of Ethics, 19*(4), 349–356.

Edmondson, A. C. (2012). *Teaming: How organizations learn, innovate, and compete in the knowledge economy*. Jossey-Bass.

Harris, H., & Sandhu, S. (2017). Effective use of reflection and research activities in teaching business ethics. *Research in Ethical Issues in Organizations, 17*, 49–61. https://doi.org/10.1108/S1529-209620170000017008

Kolb, D. A. (1984). *Experiential learning: Experience as the source of learning and development*. Prentice-Hall.

Ladyshewsky, R. K. (2006). Peer coaching: A constructivist methodology for enhancing critical thinking in postgraduate business education. *Higher Education Research & development, 25*(1), 67–84.

Ladyshewsky, R. K. (2017). Peer coaching as a strategy to increase learning and development in organisational life-a perspective. *International Journal of Evidence Based Coaching and Mentoring, 15*(1), 4–10.

May, R. (1994). *The courage to create*. WW Norton & Co.

Palm, K., Ullström, S., Sandahl, C., & Bergman, D. (2015). Employee perceptions of managers' leadership over time. *Leadership in Health Services, 28*(4), 266–280.

Schön, D. A. (1983). *The reflective practitioner: How professionals think in action*. Basic Books.

Siegel, D. J. (2020). *The developing mind: How relationships and the brain interact to shape who we are* (3rd ed.). The Guilford Press.

Wilke, G. (2014). *The art of group analysis in organisations. The use of intuitive and experiential knowledge*. Karnac.

Index

C. Sandahl, M. von Knorring, *Managing with Sense and Sensitivity*,
https://doi.org/10.1007/978-3-031-24109-3

MIX
Papier aus verantwortungsvollen Quellen
Paper from responsible sources
FSC® C105338

If you have any concerns about our products,
you can contact us on
ProductSafety@springernature.com

In case Publisher is established outside the EU,
the EU authorized representative is:
Springer Nature Customer Service Center GmbH
Europaplatz 3, 69115 Heidelberg, Germany

Printed by Libri Plureos GmbH
in Hamburg, Germany